“*Delta Blues* is a vivi
and insecurity, but v
light and life. It is al
of death handed dov
yourself revealed in i
gods which have controlled you for too long.”

James S. Woodroof, Author, Teacher and Mentor

“Yes” breathes on every page of *Delta Blues*. Emerging from the difficult family life in which he grew up, emerging from his personal struggle to find his real self, emerging from encounters with failure, Terry kept saying “Yes.” And that fierce commitment to “Yes” eventually brought him home to himself, his family, and others.”

Landon Saunders, President of Heartbeat, Inc.

“*Delta Blues* reveals the crushing soul-wound of early tragedy and the long process involved in finding wholeness.”

Larry Malone, Pilot of A-6 Intruder during the Viet Nam War, Retired Navy Captain

“This book holds a key to healing unseen hurts. It will inspire you to be more honest and compassionate with yourself and others.”

Norma Sarvis, Teacher, Mentor and Leader of Youth in Jerusalem, Israel

“*Delta Blues* is hard to put down. I found it so close to my own story that at some points I wept. It’s a powerful story, full of good news and well told. The questions in the Appendix were particularly helpful.”

Brown Kinnard, Spiritual Director, Retired Chaplain Supervisor and Seminary Professor

“*Delta Blues* is one man’s incredibly honest recounting of how he became a mess. But it’s more, thank God. It’s also a story of discovery and redemption.”

Steve Holt, Sr., Writer

"Who do you look to when your family has splintered into a thousand pieces, leaving you filled with a deep sense of betrayal, loss, and confusion? How do you live in wholeness and joy in spite of many wrong turns and false starts? And once you have found your way, how do you deal with the inner voices that say you are worthless unless you are caretaking someone else? *Delta Blues* is the story of grace extended and, ultimately, of grace received. It is the story of hope."

Cindy McMillan, Teacher and Author

"*Delta Blues* chronicles the healing and joy that result from honest and persistent attention to one's personal reality and the personal realities of others. Terry Smith's story shows the process of reflection and contemplation leading from brokenness and pain to awareness and wholeness."

F. Joseph McLaughlin, Ph.D., Vanderbilt University
Professor of Psychology and Child Psychologist

"Many capable business executives get into trouble because of unconscious but compelling codes of personal conduct that did not match the reality of their lives or circumstances. In the compelling personal narrative of *Delta Blues*, Terry Smith reveals how difficult it is to get in touch with privately held beliefs that rule one's perception of the truth."

Ronald G. Joyner, MHA, Life Fellow,
American College of Healthcare Executives

"*Delta Blues* tells the story of everyone. We all have unconscious childhood solutions for our problems that end up sabotaging us as adults. What's great about this book is that it is the real thing. It's not a book about a quick fix; it's a book about the real fix that takes place over a lifetime of honest struggle."

Russell Bloodworth, Jr., Executive Vice President
of Boyle Investment Company, Memphis

Delta Blues

From DARKNESS to Light

Terry S. Smith
with Craig Borlase

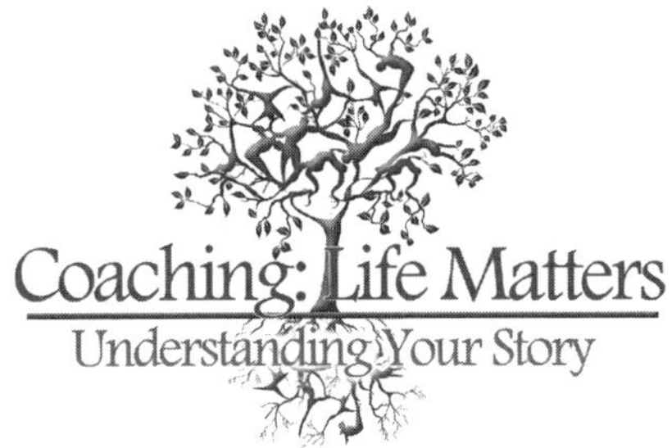

Delta Blues is a true story—my story, but I have tried to protect the identities of several people mentioned in the book. The facts are correct; the names have been changed for the sake of privacy.

To order copies of this book, please e-mail
www.coachinglifematters.org.

Cover design by Karen Roof, and book design by Gary Gore.

Printed in the United States of America

To my granddaughters
Sydney, Aubrey Anne, Maia, Averil, and Olivia;

my grandsons
Wallace, Preston, Peter, Sterling, and Isaac;

and my daughters
Sara, Melissa, Margaret, and Elizabeth

In memory of Liz LaVelle and Ty Osman II

Contents

From the Author

As my search for real life began, hope entered in a gentle and quiet way, and I had to travel a journey from darkness to light. I will take you back to my beginning.

As you enter the sacred halls of my life, you will enter your own. Don't be afraid! Over the last forty years I have listened to literally ten thousand life stories. Many far worse than mine. I have met courageous, overcoming people. *You are an amazing person. You can figure out your life.* With good information, time, and a safe place you can think through anything. *It is never too late.*

How to Use This Book

Questions for each chapter are provided in Appendix A. The questions were crafted by Jean Enochs, PhD in biology, nurse practitioner, former professor at the University of Michigan, and initiator of medical health care clinics that are run by trained local people within the culture of Belize. She is also a trained spiritual mentor.

These questions will create discussion for groups and individuals as they reflect on their own stories and share with others their insights and learnings. The answers to these questions are important in a confidential group where people are gathered in a safe atmosphere with respect and love. Richness and wisdom are found in people's stories as they reflect on their personal journeys. This will provide a place to grow in deeper genuine love for the people in your world.

Foreword

I have known Terry Smith for forty years and have walked with him through much of the time he was struggling to understand himself as he peeled off the toxic layers of his past that were plaguing him in his all-out efforts to serve others while, at the same time, trying to save himself and serve his family. I was with him in Boston when he finally busted the hitch on the wagon he was so determined to pull. But that revelation was only glimpsed intellectually; the gut-wrenching reality of surrendering to it was yet to reveal itself over the next twenty years of his life.

In *Delta Blues* Terry describes his journey as going from darkness to light. Reading this called to my mind an incident reported in a newspaper:

> On a December day some years ago, a Florida lawyer with a love for salt water attempted to surpass the free-diving record of five years standing. With the aid of an artificial lung strapped to his back, he began the descent. It was off the coast of Miami. At 306 feet below the surface, he topped the record for anyone who had returned alive. Still further he dropped to 350 feet, then 400, surpassing now the record of a French diver who had lost his life in the attempt. At this point instruments aboard the surface ship showed that he hesitated, then, instead of coming up, he began to descend again! Somewhere below 550 feet he set a record but lost his life in the murky depths.
>
> Why did he fail to turn back? One guess is that he lost a sense of direction within the blackness. Another plausible answer is that he succumbed to what the French free-diving fraternity calls the "rapture of the depths." "The rapture of the depths" is a kind of intoxication of pressure and blackness which lures its unfortunate victim past the point of safe return. This is a symbol of what can happen in a person's life. This is what happened to our young man.

Delta Blues mirrors that story—with one giant difference: Terry began his ascent to light and life. Having come out of the depths of the toxic waste of his turbulent childhood, Smith now returns at great risk to those murky waters to attempt the rescue of other victims who have lost their sense of direction and are on the verge of losing their lives. *Delta Blues* is a story of victory over the "hidden gods" that we unconsciously allow to control our lives.

Terry's victory, chronicled in this book, also calls to mind lines from a poem by Owen Seaman:

> *Tell your sons [and daughters] who see the light*
> *High in the heavens, their heritage to take:*
> *"I saw the powers of darkness put to flight!*
> *I saw the morning break!"*

Delta Blues is a vivid record of a child who was raised in the darkness of fear and insecurity but overcame the darkness and was raised to light and life. It is also a love story that breaks the relational cycle of death handed down from generations. You may very well find yourself revealed in its pages and thus be freed from the unconscious gods that have controlled you for too long. Being freed, you can say to your children, "I saw the powers of darkness put to flight! I saw the morning break!"

James S. Woodroof

Prologue

It is March, and the air is cold. What little warmth there is can be felt only when standing in the light of the sun. Move out of its rays, and the chill sets in straightaway. I choose to stand in the shadow of the church. I choose to feel the cold.

This is not the first funeral I have been to this year, nor will it be the last. But this will be the one that leaves the deepest marks. Most of the friends I have buried of late have been men who have lived long lives and whose eyes have gently faded with the passing years. Their funerals have been marked not by a sense of shock or trauma but by a sense of gratitude. They have been times to tell stories, to dig deep into the wealth of tales that come from lives lived fully and lives lived long.

All of us here, arms hunched against the cold, holding ourselves tightly to preserve the warmth, know this funeral is different. All of us who are here for Ty Osman II know this life was too short. We meet to mark the passing of a young man who died just five days earlier in a tragic car accident. Though there were decades between us, he was my friend. For all of us, he was our friend, and not one of us was ready to see him go.

This is not a book about death, although there are funerals and tears to be found within these pages. This book is about life. Partly, it is a book about my life—how I grew up at the intersection between sorrow and joy, how I experienced rejection and acceptance, how I became a man blessed so wonderfully by faith, family, and friendship. But this book is also about other stories than my own. It is a book about ordinary people who chose to make the leap and trust God to lead them. Where? Away from the pain and troubles toward real life—the infectious sort that intrigues and attracts and inspires others. Lives just like the life of Ty II.

There is a song that says, "Forget your perfect offering. There is a crack in everything." In many ways that is just what this book is about: recognizing what is broken in life and deciding not to let it limit us. Instead this book is about allowing the broken to make us stronger, to make us brighter and better. That's the way it happened for so many people. All of these stories of transformation are just a reflection of the best story of them all: the life, death, and resurrection of the man known as Jesus of Nazareth. It is because of his story that I can tell my own. It is because of what he went through that each of us can step forward today. It is because he was broken that his light now shines fully.

It really is time to move out from the shadow and go into the church now. In my hand has been placed a guide to the service. There, sandwiched between four songs that will fill the building with words about grace, about singing in spite of the closing darkness, about giving everything to God and how he is above even death itself, I see these words and my name:

Celebration of Life—Terry S. Smith

I have so much to celebrate in my life—enough to fill a hundred services like this. But dear Ty II's life was so short compared to mine. Can I overcome the sorrow enough to do it justice? What can I, a man who has already breathed his threescore and ten, say about Ty II's life?

I can say that I saw in him a life filled with joy. He may have seen only eighteen summers, but he had moved from despair to hope.

I can say that even though he lived short, he lived full.

I can say that, perhaps more than anyone I have ever known, he let the light in.

Ty II's world was stopped with his sudden *physical* death. My world was stopped as a child with *relationship* death. *Is there an answer that makes sense that deals with these two devastating losses?*

PART ONE

No one ever told me that grief felt so like fear.

—*C. S. Lewis*

CHAPTER ONE

I Am Born and I Am Loved

1942–1949

WHEN I FELL from the attic through the empty shell of the unfinished house onto the compacted earth far below, I should have been unable to get up. My six-year-old body should have been seriously hurt by the fall. Broken bones, internal bleeding, and some kind of trauma to my little blond-topped head—any one of them could have left me pinned to the floor. And yet the fall didn't get me. My friends did. They scooped me up and placed me in their red wagon that they had lined with old sacks left behind by the builders. Glenn, Tommy, and Pee Wee pulled hard to drag me up Frank Street to my home. And when they had done that and it was clear that I was well, we all ran back outside again to carry on with our games.

Memphis, 1948. Frank Street was our playground. We'd play cork ball under the big oak tree using a broom handle for a bat and a cork wrapped in tape for the ball. We'd play king of the hill, left field ball, capture the flag, and almost break our necks trying to impress the high school football coach who lived down the street. We'd show off our passing skills right there in front of his house, but he was never at home to see us. My older brother, Sid, and I were close but fought often, and most of the time I lost, especially when he figured out how to flush my head down the commode. But one day I turned on him and fought back. He never did it again.

Ours was a blue-collar neighborhood. Jobs were plentiful after the war and the local firms made tires, elevators, and a whole bunch more. People weren't rich, but they weren't poor either. Still, I guess my family had a little more than others. Ours was the only house with a television. On Monday nights we crowded around to watch the wrestling, all wide-eyed and awed by the wrestlers' strength. In late afternoons we'd be riveted to the screen, watching thrilling episodes of *The Lone Ranger* and *Hopalong Cassidy*. All of us were there, ten or more of us neighborhood kids—mostly boys—faces lit up by that tiny monochrome screen.

My parents were kind to let the other kids watch our TV, but that was not at all unusual for the neighborhood. Everybody was friendly, and though we were in the city of Memphis, we felt that we were our own little town because of the way the river and woods bordered the area. Wherever you were, there was someone to watch out for you or to inform your parents if you had been up to no good.

One family was particularly special to me. The Everett Roseberry family had seven kids of their own; the youngest was Glenn, and they knew me as Bubba. They say I reminded them of little Glenn and that's why they were so kind, but I think they were placed there by God himself to show me just what a good and loving family should look like.

Pa Roseberry was the custodian of the school, which gave the family certain privileges. They got a house with bills paid, and the scraps from the school cafeteria were theirs to give to the chickens. But we loved the land the most. After the teachers had gone home, it wasn't the school's playground; it was ours. Everything that mattered in life happened on or around that playground, and kids came from ten blocks away to compete in our cork ball tournaments and play in the open field.

But this is only part of my story. If my childhood contained just the Roseberrys and Frank Street and Monday night wrestling and cork ball tournaments, this story would be very different. My story does not really start here on Frank Street. My story starts earlier, behind the closed doors of the only house on the street with a TV. My home was owned by a pair of teenagers, two people freshly married who had a family growing before their eyes. As I began my childhood, my parents were still living out their adolescence. Neither of them was at all equipped for adulthood, much less for marriage or child rearing. How could they have been?

"My parents were still living out their adolescence."

When they married, my father, Sid, was the older and

wiser one, but he was just nineteen. His first two decades had been tough. Sid was two years old when his own father died, and it was up to his mother to parent him completely. She was an orphan and received only a third grade education. With no training and no husband, her options were limited. She worked in a department store dipping candy into chocolate until she was eighty-five. She gave Sid whatever he wanted, never seeing any wrong in any of his actions, yet Mama Etta was a kind, strong, and loving person. Daddy might not have had much in the way of positive male role models, but at least in his mother he could see some of the hallmarks of love. And Mama Etta, committed as she was to church and church attendance, made sure that her only son—and later my siblings and me—attended every week. For me, church was a warm and loving place. Unfortunately, Daddy ceased regular attendance as a teenager because he found church constricting, rigid, and irrelevant.

Mama came from wealth, and she came from trouble. Both parents were well educated, and that side of my family tree is well covered with lawyers and doctors and other upstanding icons of success. Mama started out life on a plantation in Tennessee; her home was like Tara in *Gone with the Wind.* At one time in our sad history the family owned one hundred slaves and lived like royalty, but by the time Mama's parents, Claude and Lucy Ann Jones, took over, their wealth was long gone.

Grandma Jones was raised a Methodist, and her husband, Claude, was a Campbellite—a group of religious fundamentalists who believed that they alone were going to heaven. My grandfather was broken by a series of tragic losses; his first wife and baby died in childbirth, and his second wife, Lucy Ann, bore triplets, who also died. My grandfather's younger brother had just graduated from medical school when he shot himself on a riverboat after getting a "Dear John" letter from his girlfriend. My grandfather medicated his pain with alcohol, beginning a cycle of death that impacted all of our lives.

First, he gambled away his mercantile store. Then, in 1927, when Mama was just four years old, the plantation house burned to the ground. It appears that was the point at which her mother decided to take control, and having bought a new, large house, she provided a living for the family by taking in boarders. My alcoholic grandfather was left to deal with the children, and he was incapable of ever saying no. There were fights and tears and all manner of heartaches until, eventually, he died four years before my birth when Mama was fifteen.

In the days before my grandfather passed, he repented of all the wrong he had done his family. Yet the damage was done, and Mama's two brothers died as alcoholics. The house was the last thread connecting Mama's family with their former glory. And like that broken-down house, the whole family history is peppered with violence, alcoholism, and sorrow. A stupor hung over this wing of my family, and Mama was no exception.

Lucy Mildred, my mother, was the youngest of four children, and her parents were old when she was born. Perhaps it was having a forty-seven-year-old mother and a fifty-three-year-old father that led her to want to start a family while she was so young.

As a girl, Mama was pursued by many young men. Three of them had declared their love for her, and the choice was hers to make. I understand Mama could not make up her mind which one she wanted to marry. In the end she chose Daddy, although I do not know why. Perhaps it was love. Perhaps it was because he would not take no for an answer.

Her mother, Grandma Jones, was a wise money manager and saved enough to purchase a small house for nineteen-year-old Sid and sixteen-year-old Mildred on Frank Street as a wedding gift. My grandmother's act of generosity allowed my parents to move from teenage sweethearts to a ready-made family unit—only they didn't quite have the children. However, within nine months of the wedding my brother Sid was born. Both grandmothers stepped in to help, rescuing Mama in the process. I came along nineteen months after that, followed sixteen months later by my sister Carol. Three children, and Mama was only twenty years old, still dependent on her mother and my father for endless practical and emotional support.

Having their own home was better than being given daddy's car keys for the night, and Sid and Mildred goofed off like the children they were. There were *five* childhoods in play at our house by the time my sister Carol arrived.

Both grandmothers lived nearby, and Mama Etta came every day after work to help with the children. The Roseberry family across the street was another source of support. Meantime, my parents' friends hung out at our house, and Daddy ran with his buddies in the evening, leaving the care of the children to my teenage mother, the grandmothers, and helpful neighbors.

Mama played with us like any child would play with her dolls. When she got tired of playing, she just walked away. The grandmothers, other relatives, and neighbors took up the slack. Mama seemed to relish playing the role of child. Perhaps she resented us for taking her place, but whatever the cause, the effect was clear. She was unable to look after us. She relied on the grandmothers to know when to change a diaper and what to feed us.

"My grandmother's act of generosity allowed my parents to move from teenage sweethearts to a ready-made family unit."

The fact that the nation was at war increased the difficulties. Daddy joined the Navy in 1944, adding to the pressure at home. He was not away that long, compared to some kids' dads. First, he broke his ankle in boot camp. Then in 1945 he was discharged because he had three children at home. Yet even though he stayed in the States, we didn't see him while he was in the service.

Left with three children under three years old, Mama was unable to cope. Not long after Carol was born, my twenty-year-old mother had a mental breakdown. I learned this from Ina Roseberry years later. She told me that Mama's depression made her so unstable that she planned to take our lives and then kill herself. Did Daddy know? I am still unsure. But I do know that when he returned, things got worse.

One critical time was an evening in May 1947. I was almost five years old. My parents had friends over for a party. During the evening, Mama observed Daddy heading out into the backyard with her best friend. It was obvious what they were going to do. In retaliation, Mama slept with Daddy's best friend. This was the start of a secret that remained uncovered for almost three decades, yet the additional damage it caused my parents' marriage was felt much, much sooner. As my parents gave in to the toxic hatred that followed the party, our family began to collapse. People took sides, and the situation grew worse.

My main support came from across the street. The Roseberrys were always warm and loving to me. In contrast, my home was becoming a place of feuds, bitterness, and open hostility. Even though the Roseberrys were critical of Daddy for failing to help out with us as much as they felt he should have, and even though Daddy resented their increasing outspoken concern, I was a constant Roseberry visitor. So much so that I have few memories of Mama from those days, although I do have many of Mrs. Roseberry and her clan. When one of my daughters asked me recently if I missed Mama (who died in 2000), the only reply that I could give was that I missed the voice of Ina Roseberry Reed, the daughter of the Roseberry family.

"As my parents gave in to the toxic hatred, our family began to collapse."

By the time I was old enough to go to school, I was old enough to know that something was not right with Mama. Today, I know that she was clearly spinning out of control, but back then I was just fearful. One afternoon, she and some of her young friends dropped us children off at the movie theater. As her car pulled away, I was left with a deep feeling of abandonment. Confusion overwhelmed me; I did not know what was happening. After the picture show ended, we waited and waited for her to return to pick us up. I was five years old and terrified. We were lucky that a kind man saw our predicament and stayed with us until Mama and her friends finally came to get us. Mama might have been pretty, smart, and humorous, but she was preoccupied with things other than us. Even at our young ages, all of us knew that.

One afternoon my brother Sid and I got caught smoking behind the garage, and Mama brought us back into the house.

"Y'all don't need to hide your smoking," she said. "You can smoke in front of us." With that, she opened a pack of cigarettes and offered us one. When we finished the first, she gave us another and then another and another. Eventually we were very sick. I was just six years old, and I never smoked again. Perhaps it was not the most foolish thing she ever did, but on reflection today I find that her actions sadden me.

For every incident when things went wrong at home, there were a hundred more examples of love and acceptance from the Roseberrys. With them I felt favored and cherished. Thanks to them, my early childhood had many of the essentials that my parents were unable to provide.

The older brothers taught me how to play ball, fight, and enjoy life. They taught me how to throw newspapers every afternoon, first folding them in just the right way so that they would sail from the street to the doorstep. They taught me their songs—one about looking over a four-leaf clover—and we were always singing, always playing, always working together, and always going full speed. At the Roseberrys I felt safe, secure, and beloved by their whole family. Ina Roseberry, the family's only daughter, carried me around on her hip, and when my youngest brother, Robert, was born, Ina and her new husband, Tink, cared for me while Mama was even less able to cope than she had been before. They played games with me, and I felt Ina's delight and the pleasure she took in my presence. Hers was the voice of the nurturing female I so desperately needed.

Eating peanut butter and jelly sandwiches, listening to the ball game or boxing match on the radio, being held close by Mrs. Roseberry, taking a bath in their kitchen sink until I was big enough to graduate to the bathtub, following Glenn around as he carried out his chores, singing all the time—these are some of the best memories I hold from my childhood.

On the other side of the street, my home life was becoming increasingly difficult. Daddy worked for DuPont, so we had enough money for food and other necessities. His good job also provided funds for my parents' parties. My memory tells me they were getting out of hand at that time. One evening, a man who was a friend of Daddy painted himself black and covered his mouth with bright red lipstick. He burst through our back door with a rifle in his hands pointed right at us. We screamed in terror while he laughed in delight. That fear was deep and difficult to shake; I felt a pressure on my chest. Who could know what would happen next?

My life was being defined by the extremes. On one side of

the street were love, warmth, and affection. On the other side were danger, fear, and chaos. Perhaps it was inevitable that my parents' paths would separate. Perhaps it was impossible to hope they could ever remain together as they had for those first seven years of my life.

I am not sure what followed was unavoidable, but I do know it was painful. And yet for all the tears I would cry alone in the coming weeks and months, the reality is that I was emotionally devastated during those early years. I was knocked out and traumatized. Yes, I survived, but the injury has taken a lifetime to heal. The Roseberry family provided comfort, but I've had to face the truth that I was a deeply wounded child.

"My life was being defined by the extremes."

CHAPTER TWO

I Am Alone

1949–1954

THOSE FIRST few years of my life were characterized by the two sides of the street: one offering love and acceptance and endless games filled with laughter; the other full of fear, danger, and the threat of Mama's unpredictable behavior and Daddy's absence. Yet as the war ended, Daddy returned, and life began to open up again. I faced a new trauma different from the shock of living around Mama. When I was seven, Daddy decided to move us twelve miles north and east to a middle-class Memphis suburb called Bartlett.

For a little kid like me, Bartlett might as well have been Toledo. My former world was shattered. I felt robbed of the love I received from the Roseberrys, and I did not know why this was happening. I was devastated. No one even tried to explain. They simply told me we were moving. Daddy was not only making a new start; he was also escaping the judgment he felt from the neighbors on Frank Street.

Perhaps if I had known something—anything—about what was happening, I would have been better able to cope. If I had even been allowed to say good-bye or to return to Frank Street and the warmth and love of the Roseberrys from time to time, I would have felt differently. But none of this was offered. In an instant, I was ripped away from the surrogate family who had provided me with so much support and affection, and they were never spoken of again. I guess you could say my parents were good at keeping secrets.

"I was ripped away from the surrogate family who had provided me with so much support and affection."

Now Daddy was at work, and we were home alone with Mama. I tremble inside remembering the time I got off the school bus and walked into the house to find Mama sitting on the couch and drinking wine with a man who was not my daddy. I was nauseated, ran outside, and climbed a tree. There are no words to describe the feelings crashing through me.

It was the first time I felt the full impact of the brokenness of their relationship. I had started second grade and was experiencing a kind of traumatic shock. When my teacher was speaking, she appeared to be fifty feet away from me, even though I knew she was much closer. Years later, I discovered that such an experience can indicate a person is dissociating, or *withdrawing emotionally*, as a result of external trauma.

It is hard to believe, but Daddy's job caused us to move again. Within a year, we were seventy-five miles south in the small Mississippi town of Clarksdale, an antebellum part of the Delta made famous for its decadence by William Faulkner.

Clarksdale was a test. My ability to dissociate was one way of escaping, but I needed more. We knew no one in town. Mama was out with her drinking buddies. And when she was at home, she was just not present with us. Nurturing was nonexistent. The grandmothers did not make the trip to see us there, so they were no help to us. I was getting by marginally at school, but emotionally I was hurting. I had to work hard to make friends. The relational skills I learned from the Roseberry family—the ability to play sports, the love of music and dance—were unconsciously in my survival kit, and I used them to gain a feeling of significance, affirmation, and esteem. I also started to drift closer to Daddy. I felt his helplessness and the raging, cursing hatred that spewed out of Mama's mouth. I wanted to comfort Daddy in his trauma and learn to be a good boy who would not cause him trouble. This was the beginning of an obsession that would haunt me in later years.

"My fear of abandonment was never far from the surface."

My fear of abandonment was never far from the surface. By the time I was eight and in the third grade, we returned to Memphis each weekend. One day—it can only have been weeks before my parents finally agreed to separate—we kids were acting up in some way in the backseat of the car. Sid was blamed, and I watched in horror as he shouted that he wanted out of the car. The deepest fear swept over me as Daddy pulled over and let Sid out into a cotton field. We were at least an hour away from home, and Sid—one of my precious lifelines, one of the few dependables that remained—ran away from us. *Is this how life is going to go for me? Will everyone leave until there is nothing left?* In time, Sid slowed, turned around, and came back to the car, but the panic took a long time to leave my system.

After that the family dramas escalated with out-of-control drinking, cursing, and open hostility in our home. It was there that the final curtain dropped. I remember the day we three older children, crying and terrified, stood in the front yard. Daddy was holding Robert in his arms. In front of us was a car parked at the curb, the engine running. In it were drinking buddies of Mama. They had already helped load her suitcases and were watching as my parents argued on the sidewalk.

"Mildred," shouted Daddy, "if you get in that car and leave, don't ever come back!" Defiantly, she slid into the backseat and left. We stood there traumatized. Mama was twenty-six years old. She was gone, not to return. Sid was nine, I was eight, Carol was seven, and Robert was two. Everything was falling apart.

Daddy's response was to pack us up and take us back to Memphis. There was no way he could care for the four of us and still work his job in Clarksdale. In Memphis, we children were farmed out to relatives. Carol moved in with Mama Etta; Sid moved in with Dad's stepsister, Myrtle, and her husband; and Robert and I were taken in by Daddy's first cousin, Bobby Roll, and his wife, Dorothy.

We entered a new phase. Daddy came back from Clarksdale every weekend, gathered up the three older children, and headed to Mama Etta's. We played mumbley peg, where you had to throw a pocketknife into the ground and hit a stick. If you were the farthest away, you got down on your knees with your hands behind your back and pulled the stick all the way out of the ground with your teeth. We played with our BB guns and enjoyed Mama Etta's delicious, home-cooked meals.

"Children are the world's greatest recorders, but they are the world's worst interpreters."

They say children are the world's greatest recorders, but they are the world's worst interpreters. To my mind, the facts spoke for themselves: the Roseberrys were dead to me, and I had been ripped away from love. Even though my life was more stable at the Rolls' home, I was still living in an internal world of confusion, chaos, emotional abandonment, and desperation. If it hadn't been for the love and warmth I had experienced with the Roseberrys during those first seven years, I am not sure how I would have ended up. Their love showed me that there was an alternative to the darkness and despair. *If only I could find it.*

The way I gained power in my world over the next few years was simple. I was silent and tried to appear strong, even when I was crumbling inside. If I got into a fight at school, I launched the first punch, and typically there was no need for a second. In public I was strong, not weak. There was no room for crying—at least not in public. In private, it was a different story.

Being playful ended when I was seven. Not that I did not want to play, but I was too busy trying to survive. I continued to call on the survival skills I learned on Frank Street, but all along I was running on empty, at a great loss internally. I needed more of that family love and affection, but there was a drought in Memphis and Clarksdale. What little warmth and affirmation I could get from my father, teachers, or friends seemed handed out in miniature portions.

"Being playful ended when I was seven."

I can remember only one moment of real fun, although even that speaks to my sense of loneliness and abandonment. I was in the second grade, and the Walt Disney movie *Dumbo* was being shown in the school auditorium. I remember identifying so strongly with this outcast creature, the flying elephant with the big ears, that was having such a hard time being accepted. No one understood him, and he felt abandoned by his friends. His sadness was mine, but joy filled me when things changed for him. It was like we had a connection of understanding between us, and I felt a comfort I could not articulate. His big ears became his greatest asset, but my troubles at home were a long way from turning around.

Mama's mental health deteriorated, and I remember the day I was taken to visit her. It was the first time I had seen her since she left us. I looked out the window as the massive red brick building came into view. These days I know it was most likely built in the

1920s, but back then, as a child, the hospital seemed to have been there forever. Those bricks looked immovable, and those twelve steps up to the main doors seemed designed to discourage anyone to visit. The nurses wore battle-dress uniforms and neat white caps. I probably should be able to remember who was with me. After all, I was eight or nine years old. But that part of my mind is a blank. I remember only the steps, the nurses, and Mama.

Life had all but destroyed Mama, although I did not know much about that then. All I knew was that I was visiting with her in a strange-looking building somewhere an hour or two outside Memphis. A nurse showed me and, I guess, whoever had brought me there to an open area where Mama sat. She was wearing a plain dress. I observed her closely, for that was just about all I was able to do. There was no connection between us; no life, no love. Just a child sitting with a woman, wrapped up in a plain dress, locked inside her pain.

In the years that have passed I have learned to fill in the gaps in my knowledge about Mama. I have learned how she underwent electroconvulsive therapy at the hospital. I have learned about her attempting suicide through the years, spending time in and out of mental hospitals, and cutting her wrists and throat in the bath, only to be found by her alcoholic brother. I have learned about the time when she threw herself out of a car at full speed, and the time she cut her wrists while on the phone with my sister. Eight-year-old Carol was living with Mama Etta. She listened in horror as our mother told her what she was going to do before she did it. She cut; she screamed; she talked. She cut; she screamed; she talked some more. Carol listened as the blade went into her wrists and throat. It was years before Carol would talk to anyone on the phone again, and for a long time afterward, she hid whenever Mama came around.

Mama's ill health ripped into our lives at other times. Not long after the divorce, Sid, Carol, Robert, and I were out with Daddy, and Mama appeared from nowhere, pulled up to the curb, snatched three-year-old Robert, and tried to flee. Daddy was too quick for her and wrestled Robert back while keeping us all away from the sidewalk. Mama refused to give up, jumped onto the hood of Daddy's black '49 Ford, and kicked in half the windshield as we stood there watching. With every kick came a new curse, sending him to hell with nothing but pure hatred streaming from her lips. Daddy stood his ground, silent. Eventually, she gave up and left with the man who drove her there. My feelings were so deep, so sad, I had no language to express them, and nobody helped me make sense of what was happening.

Years later, my relationship with Mama underwent such a dramatic transformation that I still find it hard to believe, but this is my last memory of her from my childhood. I am told that I visited her once a few years later, but I recall no images or feelings that help me reconstruct the scene. All I have is her acting out and bringing violence and hatred down onto the windshield and Daddy.

By the time I was nine the divorce was final, and Mama was no longer actively troubling the family. I was still living with the Roll family in Memphis. Dorothy Roll, Bobby's wife, was a kind and giving person, and I felt safe and cared for in their home. I walked the four blocks to school from their house. On the weekends Sid, Carol, and Daddy joined us. We went to the movies for a double feature and cartoons. The chance to escape to a better world was irresistible. I loved the westerns as well as the comedy movies. Dean Martin and Jerry Lewis, Bud Abbott and Lou Costello, and others filled my eyes. I remember the life of the Great Caruso, the opera singer whose voice inspired so many. I loved his story and found myself singing as I walked back and forth from school. Those songs and those movie-inspired dreams gave me comfort and hope that a better life was possible.

Looking back, I can see that my parents' toxic relationship eventually separated me from many of the people who had cherished, loved, and nurtured my soul during my earliest years. I had no time to grieve those losses or even to name them. My siblings and I were tossed about like so many broken dolls, adjusting as best we could to the many moves, the new schools, the new neighborhoods, and the new faces at the table. My safest, happiest place with the Roseberrys was long gone. This was not just my first encounter with the death of relationships but also a premature end to my childhood. Ideally, a child can rely on his or her parents to provide distraction, affirmation, insight, and love, but I was left to fend for myself. The movies, my jobs, and the songs of a man I would never meet became my sources of hope and guidance.

A year or two passed, and Daddy moved me into a boarding house with him in Clarksdale. Sid, Carol, and Robert were still living with relatives in Memphis. At twelve years of age, I got my first job working in a restaurant called Little Joe's. I could hardly see over the counter, but I acted as both waiter and cook. An early morning paper route was added to my daily routine. This modest structure in my life helped mitigate my internal pain and provided a sense of accomplishment. Since then, I have never been without a job. My childhood was over.

"My story is a story of hope. My story is a story of discovery. My story is about breaking the cycle of death."

My story is a story of hope. My story is a story of discovery. My story is about breaking the cycle of death. My family history is punctuated by alcoholism and abuse, suicide and despair, and by the sense that doom and chaos are inevitable. As a child I suffered but not without hope. I think the early years of love and support I experienced left me with a longing and hope for the future—even the false hope that Mama and Daddy would come back together. It was hard to imagine, but I prayed that we all would be reunited.

Why could my parents not figure out how to love? What was so hard about providing a place of peace and joy for their children to discover the greatness of life? My parents were unable or unwilling to rise above their hurts and traumas, passing their warped view of the world onto me. In the decades that have followed my childhood, I have tried to understand not just my own story but also that of my parents. In time I shall share with you some things I have discovered, but for now, I close with the simple idea that all was not as I thought it was. As I have reflected on the chaos and confusion, I have been able to find moments of light, significant encounters, a song in the night, a vision of dawn breaking, a longing for love, and a searching heart looking for something more that makes sense. The longing, seeking, and hungering gave me the questions that I followed. The pursuit of those questions—*the hope that I could find answers*—allowed me to take the first steps away from a place of despair toward something worth living for.

But it is the spirit in a person,
the breath of the Almighty,
that gives them understanding.

It is not only the old who are wise,
not only the aged who understand
what is right.

—*Job 32:8–9*

CHAPTER THREE

I Am Not Safe Here

1954–1960

EACH YEAR seemed to bring a new school and a new home. In the first grade I was on Frank Street, but in the second grade we moved out of the city to Bartlett. By the third grade we were in Clarksdale, but I spent the fourth grade back in Memphis living with my uncle and aunt. Fifth grade saw me back in Clarksdale living in the boarding house with Daddy.

What does this kind of movement do to a child? In a way, the fresh starts were opportunities for me to practice my survival skills—being friendly, warm, and kind, dancing and singing with freedom, but also being ready to stand up for myself if I needed to. In the fifth grade a big guy was bullying me. We almost started fighting on the playground, but I guess we knew that we would get in trouble if we chose such a public place to deal with our issues. So we arranged to fight a few blocks away on the corner after school. I was nervous as I waited there, but the guy didn't show. It was an easy victory. Those Roseberry boys were tough kids, and they taught me how to fight and win.

But who am I kidding? Although I liked the one-on-one time with Daddy in Clarksdale, life was rough. I was no longer with my brothers, sister, and Mama Etta, and I missed them terribly. On weekends we met up, but it was never quite right. We never saw Grandma Jones after the divorce. Too many hard feelings were there, and Daddy would not take the chance that we would run into Mama. Anytime he even spoke of Mama, a vein bulged in his neck.

"We never saw Grandma Jones after the divorce."

For the next two and a half years Daddy and I shared a room in a series of boarding houses. Daddy was getting older, and his increasing maturity gave me a sense of stability. He was a field engineer working on machines in banks around the state, and I was old enough to walk to whatever school I was attending.

In class, I was able to keep up with the math, but I struggled with reading comprehension. I was in the bottom third of my class, but it didn't matter all that much to me. I'd stroll home, singing as I went, check in with whatever landlady we were staying with at the time, and wait until Daddy came home before heading out to Little Joe's for hamburgers. We spent the weekend traveling back and forth to Memphis. I just looked forward to the reunion with my siblings and Mama Etta.

Daddy was not a talker. I could tell that he was proud of me, but we didn't talk much. We slept in the same bed, and I periodically wet it. But he was always kind and never spoke in a disparaging way. There was not much positive affirmation, but after all those years spent with Mama's chaos creating tempestuous storms, there was enough time to just be quiet together. We sometimes got up at four in the morning to go to Moon Lake and fish. I'd sit in the middle of the boat, and Daddy and his friend would be on either side. There was not much to say, and it was perfect.

He was gentle, not prone to rages and roller-coaster moods like Mama. I remember his singing. His songs invited me to join him in his "air-o-plane" and fly around Venus and Mars or warn me about the dangers of getting too drunk and mistaking a milk cow for a coat rack. He sang the same songs he sang in the Navy, and few of them were suitable for my young ears. His singing soothed me. Perhaps the one that I remember best of all is this, and it was very different from his Navy songs:

I come to the garden alone
While the dew is still on the roses
And the voice I hear falling on my ear
The Son of God discloses

And he walks with me and he talks with me
And he tells me I am his own.
And the joy we share as we gather there
None other has ever known.

When he was a young teenager, Mama Etta arranged for Daddy to lead the singing at church from time to time, and as an adult, he still had a great singing voice. He crooned like Sinatra, a sensation then, and the whole room seemed to be made a degree warmer. Daddy had such a happy presence. I adored him!

How excited I was when Daddy introduced the idea that he was going to get married again. He and I were driving to Memphis, and he asked me what I thought about his marrying Mary, a woman he met through his work. I'd met Mary, and I liked her. Compared to my birth mother, she was perfect. She seemed kind and affectionate toward me, and she even let me drive her little Nash Rambler car once. A pretty lady with an inviting smile, she worked as the cashier at the Wonder Bread Bakery Company. What twelve-year-old boy wouldn't approve? I thought, *Finally my brothers and sister can move to Clarksdale to live with us, and we can be a family once again.*

At age twenty-five Mary was already a widow. Life had left her scarred, but none of us knew that before she and Daddy married. We kids just thought we were getting a new mother. In some ways we were right. Mary's problems might have been different from Mama's, but she brought with her a world of rage and depression.

I longed for a united, happy family, but when Daddy and Mary returned from their honeymoon, Mary flew into a rage because I used her wedding towels to bathe our new puppy. All hell broke loose, and I was not allowed to keep the puppy.

It soon became apparent that Mary was insecure, seeing us children as rivals for our father's affection. Her jealousy kicked in even more strongly when the other three children moved to Clarksdale: no more fishing with Daddy, no time alone with him. There were only pouting, anger, and false accusations from her. She viewed any time we spent with Daddy, and she was not present, as a threat, as if we were conspiring against her. And so, the unspoken rule was that we children should stay clear of her as much as possible. This angry, untrusting, hardworking, mean, and unforgiving woman set the temperature for the entire house with either her raging anger or her suffocating depression. As a result, the atmosphere could be anything from tense and hostile to entirely unsafe emotionally.

Household chores were particular points of conflict. Unlike my mother, who was an alcoholic unable to act as a responsible adult, Mary became a martyr who cared for us—but only at a price. Life for her was always serious, and when she prepared a meal for us in the evening, she would not sit down and eat with us, so great was her resentment. I learned to eat fast and get out of there.

After Daddy married Mary, there were no family vacations, no eating out at Little Joe's, and no time to play together as a family. Instead we heard door slamming, arguing, and blaming someone else for the misery in her life. I stayed in the doghouse most of the time, and I was confused about why my usual happy, friendly persona didn't work with Mary. Why couldn't I get her to like me?

Daddy was not able to help me. He was passive and took a "peace at any cost" approach. Once, when Mary thought I needed a beating, he took me to the bathroom to whip me, but instead of hitting me over the backside, he brought his belt down on the commode while I yelled to add the sound effects. Another time I lost a jacket, and Daddy covered up by buying me another one. Later, when the original jacket showed up, we both got into more trouble with Mary.

Between them, Mary and Mama taught me to do whatever it took to keep my personal struggles buried deep. Throughout my teenage years I did just that, looking well and happy on the outside while dying on the inside. I might have been young, but I already had clear ideas about how I could survive.

"They taught me to do whatever it took to keep my personal struggles buried deep."

One of my jobs was to be a good boy and not cause Daddy any more pain. I learned to take responsibility for making him feel better while working my two jobs: working at Little Joe's after school and delivering papers in the morning. The income was not much, but at least I was taking some responsibility for keeping things going. Unconsciously, the pattern of feeling responsible to help others in need was strengthening in the inner recesses of my brain. Years later, instead of being a friend, it became one of my worst enemies.

I also learned how rewarding it was to perform to please others. Later, this became a dangerous obsession, but at this point, good performance earned me needed affirmation. I could sense the plight of people who were hurting, and I learned almost instinctively what to do to make them feel better and like being around me. I learned how to do that socially with friends, and I found that taking dancing lessons at school in the sixth grade gave me contact with girls. Plus, I could perform on the athletic field, tennis court, and baseball diamond.

My performances didn't always work, however. My tenth grade social studies teacher took me aside and told me that my classmates thought I was a snob. I asked her why, and she said it was because I spoke with some people and not others. My need for affirmation was so great that right away I decided to speak with a smile to every student I passed in the school hallway. The more friends I had, the better I felt about myself.

Of course, even though I had these silent strategies for navigating my world, nobody prepared me for the life changes that hit me as an adolescent, and I ended up feeling guilty, ashamed, and confused. On the inside, I felt fragmented as I tried to deal with sexual awakenings that had no place to go while having no language to express emotional and physical feelings that were welling up inside. I'm glad I didn't act out what I was feeling sexually, but I suspect the main reason I didn't was the fear of being rejected through the experience. Yet those hidden feelings and fantasies left me with terrible feelings of shame and guilt for the thoughts and desires of my heart that I felt I could tell no one.

Did church help? In a way, it did. Even with all the disruptions in my life, I attended services every week, following the pattern set by my grandmothers. My experiences in churches had been a source of comfort and support, and I felt a sense of security in that setting. Many people I met at the services were caring and believed in a loving God. When my brothers and sister moved in with us, Daddy dropped us at church on Sundays, and occasionally he attended as well.

As a young child, I had no problem believing that God especially loved little children. When I was six years old, I went to the store to get a loaf of bread. On the way home I got sleepy and stopped in the front yard of the church building near our house, lying down on the lawn with the bread as my pillow. I felt safe near the church. But it was a different story when I was a teenager. All the sexual fantasies, which I knew were wrong, left me feeling separated from God. That is, until I heard "the sermon."

It was the day the minister started talking about Jesus. He described not just the way but the reason why Jesus died. He talked about love, and I was stunned. To think that God would love me enough at my worst to actually give his life for me was almost too much to grasp.

"To think that God would love me enough at my worst to actually give his life for me was almost too much to grasp."

On that day I wept uncontrollably. I asked God to help me and to forgive me. But for what? For all the thoughts and fantasies? Sure, but it was more than that. I wanted to be put right, to be welcomed back. I wanted home, but where was that exactly? I wanted to be rid of all the mess and anger and fear and depression and betrayal that had been handed out to me by my parents. I wanted to be rid of it all, every last brick. And as I wept, I sensed that something good was happening to me.

Daddy was with me at church that day. I had never known him to be particularly religious, but he smiled and said of my baptism in the waters of God's forgiveness, "Well, we had another dunking today." To him, I suppose it was a trifle; to me, it was foundational.

No great changes in my life followed, at least not any that others could see. But something happened inside that caused me to think deeply about the love of God and the forgiveness *he* offered. Inside, I had another voice to listen to, another option to choose rather than just block things out and pretend that everything was all right.

CHAPTER FOUR

I Travel in Two Directions

1960–1962

I WAS LYING in bed when I woke up to feelings of nausea and a crippling pain sawing its way through my skull. Whose bed? Yes, it was my own. At least I hadn't fallen that far. But my head and my mouth and the fact that I was still fully clothed told me that I could not ignore the events of the previous night.

It was the start of the spring semester of 1961. I was a freshman at Ole Miss, and every Friday night I was at some fraternity party dancing to Elvis Presley, Ray Charles, James Brown (when he was with the Famous Flames), and the Platters. I knew all the rock-and-roll songs by heart and felt like I could sing them as well as Elvis. With the sun setting, I decided to get drunk. And I did. And now, alongside the waves of nausea, were even stronger tides of remorse.

As a teen, I said I would never drink alcohol. My family history had given me enough examples of its danger to warn me off. So why was I lying in bed feeling like this? The truth was that at eighteen I began to make choices that reflected my brokenness and despair. I told myself that the previous night was just a surrender to curiosity, but I was not that strong. Everything was breaking down. I was doing poorly in school, and I was doing poorly inside. The pressure was becoming too much, and I was unable to cope. I'd tried using amphetamines to help me study, but I continued to party just as hard. I was out of control. I lay there and delivered my verdict on myself: "Mama is an alcoholic, my grandfather was an alcoholic, and I guess that makes me an alcoholic."

The roots of my academic troubles did not all snake back to Mama and Daddy. In part, they were of my own making. I had no financial support other than what I could provide for myself, so I had to work. And I did. The summers before my junior and senior years in high school I worked as a playground director for the city park commission in Clarksdale, Mississippi. Monday through Friday, from nine to five, I was there caring for neighborhood children aged six to twelve. We had all kinds of games, activities, and fun crafts for the children, bringing a bit of the Roseberrys with me to the town.

After I graduated from high school, Sid was working with a crew of his college buddies in DeKalb, Illinois, laboring on pea farms, and he invited me to join them.

I felt bad for Carol left behind in that hostile environment. She was a year behind me, and I hoped she would be out of there in a year, just like me. She did graduate but married and had two children, Kirk and Mary Margaret, over the next few years. She and her family lived in Clarksdale.

Robert was twelve when I graduated, and the next six years were an even greater storm for him. It got so bad that at age sixteen he went to live with Carol.

My stepmother, Mary, had Patricia in 1958, and things got worse at home. I was just thankful to be out!

We guys worked hard on the pea farms, often more than one hundred hours spread over seven days a week. Sixteen of us lived in a bunkhouse. We were awakened every morning at 5:45 a.m. for a big breakfast before starting work in the fields at 6:30 a.m.

It was hard work. We used pitchforks to throw piles of the crop from a wagon into a machine that separated the peas from the vines. Our hands became calloused, and our bodies roasted in the sun. I've never worked so hard in my life, but the seventy-five cents an hour we earned was big money then.

By the end of the summer, I had just enough money to begin college as long as I worked thirty hours a week in the campus cafeteria. So, in part, this was my problem: how to juggle thirty hours of employment, fifteen hours of class work, and a lot of anticipated partying each week. Something had to suffer. Unfortunately, it was my classes.

"Academically, I was sinking; spiritually, I was not aware of even the presence of God."

Even when I managed to spend hours preparing for

a test, I failed. As I looked at my history grade and considered my hours of study, I wept bitterly. I made a D. Compared to others, I seemed to be failing on every front. Home had been hell, and school was not a place of refuge. I wanted to succeed, but I just could not get it together academically. My toxic beliefs, hidden inside me and unconscious, were sabotaging me. Academically, I was sinking; spiritually, I was not aware of even the presence of God. My community was my friends. I believed in God, but relationally I was bankrupt—having no family support and feeling hopeless.

"My toxic beliefs, hidden inside me and unconscious, were sabotaging me."

I tried to hold on to the one illusion I carried during this period—that I was a cool guy, a great dancer, and an Ole Miss cheerleader who was liked by the girls. It was a huge deal to be a cheerleader, but I did not have the finances to join a fraternity. My long-term friendships from high school were gone. My buddies were moving in different directions, going to other colleges or to the military, and I had no one left to confide in or to be with. Despite my illusions, I felt alone and abandoned all over again.

One evening in Oxford, I called a lovely young lady on the phone and asked her to go out with me in thirty minutes. She turned me down, and when she did, I suddenly felt the emptiness inside take one last bite. There was no language to describe how shattered this simple rejection made me feel. Despair was the only thing left inside me, and drinking helped mask the despair. But that is only one reason I was moved to drink. The other is more complicated. And it started the day my view of the Christian world fell apart.

Mama Etta had prayed on her knees for us as children. She had been such a joyful and loving person in our lives. But what about God? Where was he? Could he help me? In despair and alone in my dorm room, I picked up the Bible given to me by Dorothy Roll and began to read the story of Jesus in the book of John. It was difficult reading because it was written in King James English, but I persevered for the next three and a half hours.

As I read, one line spoken by Jesus stopped me in my tracks: "I am come that they might have life, and that they might have it more abundantly." I wanted to know what he meant. Surely this guy was a liar or crazy. Or perhaps he was telling the truth. As a little boy

I had been taught that God was good, and in this story, Jesus did good to people, yet they killed him. Was he God? And if so, how could someone who lived two thousand years ago have anything to say to me today? I wanted to know everything about him: who he was, how he put his pants on, and who his friends were. If he was real and telling the truth, I had to know.

Earlier, some students who went to a church in Oxford had befriended me. Their minister had taken me under his wing and tried to mentor me. I remember waking him up after midnight one evening for counsel as I tried to work through my love life with my teenage sweetheart. The relationship with Martha was very affirming in that I believed she cared about me above all the guys who were pursuing her. She grew up in the wealthiest family in this Delta town, and I did not know how to bring her world and my world together. I was confused and sought counsel from the minister.

He was kind and compassionate, and I quickly trusted him. But then in the fall of 1961, I received word that this mentor, minister, and friend was leaving the church; he and his wife were getting a divorce. Theirs had been a beautiful family of five, and the news was devastating. When I heard it, I felt even more hopeless. How could I hope to make it if the minister and his family could not? I had always wanted to have a family someday, and I promised I would not do to my children what was done to me. But this news left me in desolation. Could I really hope to break free?

I was losing again. One who was close and who cared could no longer offer support. I wept bitterly. There was nobody I could talk to about this. Again, I was alone and hurting, playing the record of my early childhood. As I cried, the thought came to me: *Let no man be your teacher; test everything.* I knew I could not trust Mama; I hadn't seen her in years. Daddy was relationally imprisoned in his marriage to Mary, and now my mentor and friend minister had fallen and failed. The loneliness was familiar terrain to me. I knew I needed help.

"Things that had worked in the past to numb my pain were not working."

Things that had worked in the past to numb my pain were not working. I saw in my parents' lives that their misguided efforts to escape their pain led them more deeply into the pit of death. How could I survive? What could I do? Were there answers for me? Was there any hope?

I turned again to the Scriptures I had been reading, desperate to seek solace and hope. The minister mentor had given me these words, which came to my mind: *For by these He has granted to us His precious and magnificent promises, so that by them you may become partakers of the divine nature, having escaped the corruption that is in the world by lust.*

I heard no audible voice, but somehow I knew beyond a doubt that the verses that followed contained wisdom upon which to build my entire life, adding brick by brick to build a totally new life, traveling step by step toward a better destination. In retrospect and in light of my life history, it was a near miracle that these words came to my mind. Instead of turning away from God, I moved toward him. In fact, I determined that only he would be my teacher.

"Instead of turning away from God, I moved toward him."

My heart burned for knowledge. In the fall of 1961, I was able to take a course in biblical archeology taught by Dr. Jack Lewis. He had a Ph.D. from Hebrew Union in the Hebrew Scriptures and a Ph.D. from Harvard in the New Testament. I was a first-semester sophomore at Ole Miss, still trying to fit study and employment into my life. Dr. Lewis flew into Oxford once a week to lecture for three hours. There were only three people taking the class for credit: me; Dr. Doug Shields, a physics professor; and Dean Priest, a graduate math student. One evening, during the third hour of the class, Dr. Lewis said, "I guess we had better stop the class since a third of the class is asleep."

It woke me up. Yet even though I was eager to learn, I still did not know Moses from Abraham. Of course, I flunked the class.

Life does not follow straight lines or make neat corners. My decision to trust my instincts and build up my faith bit by bit, to act well and do the right thing, did not prevent me from taking amphetamines and getting drunk. Perhaps we are all paradoxes of good intentions and human weakness, but I knew that when I stumbled again and again, something had to change. I had to get a new start.

By semester's end I decided to switch to a Christian school. My brother Sid attended Harding College in Searcy, Arkansas, before he transferred to Ole Miss. Harding came to my mind as a place where I could study about Christ for myself. (Eventually Harding College became a university, so to avoid confusion and say either college or university, I'll just use Harding to refer to the institution.) The college was a four- or five-hour drive from Ole Miss, and I called to see what I needed to do to start there the next semester. I was surprised when the president of the college happened to answer the phone. After listening to me, he asked if I needed to leave Ole Miss for disciplinary reasons.

"No," I said, "I just want to come and study the Bible."

That was enough for him, and he invited me to join the school as the next semester started. I was even more eager to learn. I signed up for three significant courses at Harding in the spring of 1962: The Life of Christ, Western Civilization, and an English literature course where I was reading Chaucer and Shakespeare. I loved all three, and my professors were delightful. The small classes suited me, and I attended chapel daily with 1,300 other college students to sing, pray, and listen to interesting lectures on current events and Christianity.

The Life of Christ was saturating me in the greatest story ever lived, while my Western Civilization class opened a window onto European history, starting with Martin Luther. When I read his biography, *Here I Stand,* and listened in awe to the professor who had lived in Germany, the history came alive. In my English course, I loved the way the lecturer made the literature and the meaning of it so real, but I had one big problem. I was reading the Middle English text without a clue about what it was saying. I failed every test, and fearing a return to my Ole Miss struggles, I went to the professor privately and asked for help. He told me that sometimes he had students who had no trouble making an A in his course, but they struggled to make an A in life. At the same time there were C students who ended up doing great things. When I graduated three years later, he stood beside me, put his arm around my shoulder, and said, "You are going to do great things in life." The D I made in his sophomore class no longer seemed to matter that much.

I turned twenty in the summer of 1962. After spending the previous two summers working in those Illinois pea fields, I was pleased to have a job with the Southwestern Company. I was to go door-to-door selling books. After training a week in Nashville, I went to Ohio with my copies of *Webster's Collegiate Dictionary, Family Medical Book, Children's Bible Story Book, Nave's Topical Bible*, and a large family Bible. I worked sixty to seventy hours a week and took only Sundays off, and on that day we had a sales meeting to prepare for the following week. We sent all the money we collected to the company each Saturday and kept what we needed to pay rent and feed ourselves.

Because I was selling Bibles, I spent a lot of time listening to people's stories about their experience with religion. I wanted to know what people thought about God, and over the four years that I worked for the Southwestern Company, I learned a lot about people. On one occasion I went to a house with a nice fence around it and children running around in the yard. A neighbor told me not to go in, but I was trained not to miss a house. I unwired the gate and wired it back as I entered. As I approached the house, a large man in blue overalls asked, "Are you a salesman?"

"Yes, sir," I answered.

He began cursing me and told me to get off his property.

I turned around to leave, but before I could make it out, he grabbed me by the neck, broke the gate open, and threw me out the gate, adding, "If you don't move a little faster, I'm going to shoot you."

I kept walking, got into my car, and drove away. Sitting outside the next house, recovering, I saw a lady sitting on her porch and shelling beans.

"Do you shoot salesmen?" I asked.

She smiled and said, "Come up on the porch."

I didn't try to sell her a thing. She told me that the man who had threatened me—Mr. B—carried a gun in his overalls, and he tied his children to a tree during an electric storm. I breathed a sigh of relief and then called the sheriff to report him. Mr. B was notorious, but most people were kind and caring.

Even though I made a fresh start at Harding, my heart remained in Clarksdale, thanks to Martha Holland. Martha had been number one on my list since the ninth grade. She had been Homecoming Queen in the ninth grade and one of those girls a lot of guys wanted to be theirs, but for some reason she chose me. Her father was a doctor, and they lived in a grand old house with pillars that backed up to the country club. They had plenty of servants and plenty of money. Martha was given a baby blue Oldsmobile for graduation, and there's no doubt that my self-esteem got an enormous boost from her interest in me.

I often realized, however, that I was way out of my depth. One night I dined with her family at the country club. I was obviously nervous and thirsty as we sat down, and I reached over to an odd-looking glass in front of me and took a large gulp of water. Everybody just stared and then proceeded to dip their fingers in these odd-looking glasses. All except Martha. She drank from hers to make me feel better.

When I left to attend Ole Miss, Martha headed off to Randolph-Macon in Virginia. She visited me before I left Oxford. She wanted to see whether the place really was as much of a party school as everybody said, but the night turned into a disaster. I had been an Ole Miss cheerleader in the past, so after the football game I took her to a party. It was being held in a big house, and as we walked in the door, I was struck with the strong feeling that I no longer belonged or wanted to be a part of what was happening with all the drinking and smoking. People were so drunk that they were stumbling and hanging on to one another. I told Martha that I was leaving and that I would wait for her in the car if she wanted to stay. Of course, she came with me.

When we got to the car, I did not know how to articulate my feelings, so I just said that I could not do this anymore. She told me that she had a migraine headache, and I took her back to the dorm. Later, I called her on the phone, but I was unable to comfort her. I knew I ruined her weekend. I'm not sure what she was expecting, but I was no longer at a point where I identified with the drinking and the sexually charged party atmosphere at the fraternity house. I could not show her the good time she was expecting. Reflecting on that moment, I see that this was the beginning of our distancing from one another.

A year later, I got word that Martha's father committed suicide. He was in financial trouble and apparently felt that the only way he could save his family was to take his life. The family received the insurance money and was able to survive financially, but his decision would impact his family for generations. Richard Hughes, a friend, drove me over to Clarksdale so I could see Martha and be with her, but again I had nothing to say. We were in her living room with a fire going, sitting in total silence. There was an emptiness I could not articulate. I held her in silence. I felt she was numb and in shock, and I was struck dumb by the tragedy. That beautiful home felt like a dark tomb of death. Her mother did not come down to speak to me as she usually did. I could feel the despair in the atmosphere. After a while, I told Martha good-bye, and I hitchhiked back to Searcy. Clarksdale was no longer my home.

PART TWO

Aim at Heaven and you will get earth "thrown in":
aim at earth and you will get neither.

—C. S. Lewis

CHAPTER FIVE

I Am Beloved

1962–1965

EVERYTHING WAS changing in my world. My academic record at Harding was headed in the right direction, and my involvement with fellow students, service projects, and sports kept me busy and disciplined. I took a course in Wisdom Literature—an introduction to Proverbs, Psalms, Ecclesiastes, and Job. I began to read Proverbs daily for insights on how Solomon looked at life. He offered direction and insight into relationships as well as practical advice on sex, money, and even how to live practically every day with joy. I tried to follow the wisdom I was discovering, and my life was soon flourishing.

"I tried to follow the wisdom I was discovering, and my life was soon flourishing."

After the death of her father, Martha moved to Memphis with her family. We still had some contact, but I could sense an emotional distance growing between us, and I certainly did not know how to communicate what was happening inside me. I believed that God loved me, and daily I meditated on his thoughts and the kind ways I was seeing him move with both compassion and forgiveness. I knew I needed a little of both for myself. I found some while singing daily with the rest of my Harding people. Standing in the midst of several hundred students singing the old hymns like "O Love That Will Not Let Me Go" ministered to my soul. Singing inspired me and spurred me on.

In the summers I sold books while continuing to strengthen and refine my growing understanding of God. Every morning, I spent time in the book of Psalms. The psalmists were nurturing my heart in ways Mama had not been able to do. The emotions that each psalm engendered often stayed with me as I went door-to-door to sell books. Again, I made enough money to pay for the next year at college, and I was finding it felt good to be responsible for my life.

As the summer before my junior year grew to a close, I came to the conclusion that I needed to tell Martha I loved her, but that I knew there was no future for us. Although she was a dear person to me, and I cared deeply for her, I could not see us being a couple over the long term. Once the summer work was over, I went to Memphis to see her. She took me to the University Club that night for dinner, and we went back to their new home and talked. I told her my thoughts about us. I was not really sure what her reaction would be. She seemed very kind and gracious and accepted what I was saying, but I didn't ask her how she felt about us. It would have been very difficult for me if she had expressed her love and affection for me. I knew this was another fork in the road, and I believed it was the right decision. Yet coming just a year after her father's death, it must have been painful for Martha.

Back at Harding, my hunger for God seemed to expand as I returned to a new semester. For the first time I felt free, excited, confident, and hopeful. I could sense God was doing something deep within me. At the age of twenty-one, I decided to live passionately for the God who loved me so much that he would give his Son to die for me. Intuitively, I knew that the only woman I would ever marry would have to be a woman who shared that passion and wanted to serve God with all her heart. I hadn't found her yet, but I knew she must be out there somewhere.

"I could sense God was doing something deep within me."

Charlotte Burkett really didn't know how beautiful she was. She was emotionally secure, socially confident, and so very different from me. She grew up on a dairy farm in Dora, New Mexico. She had been milking cows since she was ten and had the handshake to prove it. The first eighteen years of her life had been peaceful, secure, and stable. Her father's parents lived across the road, having established a homestead there in the early 1900s. Her mother's parents also lived a couple of miles down the road, and her childhood had been a loving web of parents, grandparents, uncles, aunts, and cousins who went to the same small community church. Charlotte was beloved by all. She was in the top of her class and knew what it was to have many people love and care for her. As I said, she was so very different from me.

Charlotte was not at all self-conscious. Boys had been asking her for dates since she was thirteen years old, and her popularity continued when she attended junior college ninety miles away in Lubbock, Texas. After transferring to Harding in Searcy, she made the decision to cut the ties with all of the boys she had been dating. She arrived on campus as a beauty set free and open to whatever God had ahead of her.

The first time I saw Charlotte, I was captivated. She was being greeted by a group of friends who were obviously excited to see her again, and I asked my friends who she was, but nobody knew.

A few days later, I was walking down the sidewalk with a friend when this same young lady walked by and greeted us with an enthusiastic "Hi." Again, I wanted to know who she was, and in time I found out we were taking the same class on the book of Romans. She also worked in the library, so I saw her quite often. Even though she campaigned for another fellow in the run-up to the election of junior class president, which I eventually won, we continued to build our friendship.

She was exuberant, loved people, and was kind and friendly to everyone. She was friends with people who were popular and people who would be considered outcasts. All the prestigious girls' clubs wanted her to join them, yet Charlotte chose a group of girls who were considered outsiders for her friends.

My great romantic move happened one rainy evening on the way to a student gathering we were attending. She was in front of me, walking alone under her umbrella. I handed mine to my friend and jogged up next to her, saying, "You wouldn't let a fella walk in the rain, would you?" Of course she came to my aid. I asked her to go to the college grill, bought her an ice cream, and walked her back to the dorm. Later—much later—she said that she was surprised I didn't ask her for a date that night.

When I finally asked her for a date, she said no. But it wasn't a firm no. It was more of an ask-me-again no. So I asked her the next week to hear a lecture on the nature of God.

"God is closer than the blood in your veins."

I will never forget this first date for two reasons. First, the message delivered was summed up in the statement that "God is closer than the blood in your veins." Those words drove me to my knees like no others. Second, this was the beginning of a friendship that captured my heart and drove me to prayer for guidance and peace. The more I was around Charlotte Burkett from New Mexico, the more I wanted to be with her. I remember writing in my journal: "Lord, the more I am with her, the more I want to be around her. I don't know if she is the one or not, but whoever captures this lady's heart is going to be a blessed man. I hope that man is me."

One day I asked Charlotte to go with me to a home for the elderly just off campus. We walked together and shared a special time with these older people: singing with them, reading Scripture, and just enjoying our time together. We did it again soon afterward and then again.

Some weeks later, walking back from another visit to the home for the elderly, Charlotte suggested the next time we get there thirty minutes early so we could shine the shoes of Ol' Happy, a man in his eighties who could do nothing for himself. Her thoughtfulness impressed me.

Then one evening, something devastating happened to me that had never happened before. I went to my room about 7:30 p.m. and began to feel terribly alone. I could hear the ball games outside my window and all the noise of people near me, yet within me, I could sense nothing but despair and desperation. The internal feelings were so overwhelming that I was not able to speak. I lay down on the floor, looking up at the ceiling. I had no idea what was happening to me at the time. I just groaned.

In my study of Romans, I had been reading the eighth chapter in which Paul speaks of the Spirit of God interceding for us when we have no language of our own. That verse came to my mind, as did the words "God is closer than the blood in your veins." Could it be possible that God knew and understood what was happening to me at that very point? Could I believe that?

Looking back, I now think I know what was happening. Having lived in desperation from the age of seven till I was eighteen, I had inside me a volcano of wounded feelings. I could not stop them. I felt abandoned, and yet I was also encountering new relationships with friends, with Charlotte, and with God. A collision was taking place.

"I had inside me a volcano of wounded feelings."

Did I believe that God was closer than the blood in my veins? Did I believe that God was present, that he understood and cared? I could utter only one sound: "Yes." Yes, I did believe. From that point in the evening, everything changed. I moved from the depths of despair to inexpressible, indescribable joy. What happened left in me a hunger for more, and I began to devote myself to more prayer and more Scripture reading in the days to come.

About that time I discovered Dietrich Bonhoeffer's *Letters and Papers from Prison*. Bonhoeffer wrote them while he was in a Nazi prison before being hung in April 1945, just weeks before Allied soldiers liberated the prisoners. He had been arrested for his resistance against Hitler. I was also impacted by J. B. Phillips's *Your God Is Too Small* and Viktor Frankl's *Man's Search for Meaning*. From then on, I decided that I would try to keep a journal. Inspired by these great lives, I wanted to somehow express what was happening inside me. My journaling at that point was a feeble beginning, but over the years the stillness and reflection time made my journal my best friend.

Unexpectedly, I now faced two competing emotional loves. The more I was with Charlotte, the more I wanted to be around her, and I struggled to concentrate on my studies rather than think about her. How could such a beautiful thing become such an internal problem? I did not want to risk another college failure, so I told her I was not interested in going steady with her, but I wanted to get to know her as a friend. This left her free to date other guys, and she did! One evening I told her I had to study and could not be with her. I bought her a hamburger and watched as she went out and ate it with another guy who happened to be a star basketball player. My competition seemed great, as was my temptation to despair.

Yet I could not let anyone get between me and my relationship with God. I still was out of balance internally, and I knew that my consuming thoughts about her were somehow dangerous. I knew I could not afford to base my life on another human being. I had already experienced the unending pain, the tragedy, and the destruction of being raised by parents who had no true foundation for their lives, and I was determined that my future would be different. I wanted my life and the lives of my future children to be built on Someone who would not leave us. That Someone would have to be God. Without him, I would fail, and I knew it at the very core of my being.

"I knew I could not afford to base my life on another human being."

This was a time when I really had to trust God. I was able to let go of Charlotte only because I was experiencing a higher love I was unable to articulate. I remember feeling powerless inside. The mystical sense of God's presence was very real to me. Plus, academic stress and my fear of failure were dominant forces that caused me to back away from Charlotte. I knew if I didn't get ahold of myself, I was going to bomb out. So I chose to let her go. I didn't try to explain all this to her. I didn't have language for that. I just told her I had to stop seeing her.

Of course that did not last long. After two weeks we were back together: paying visits to the old folks' home, praying together, singing together, and sharing good friends together. We were a couple, but this time there was more balance. I was no longer so intense, and that allowed our relationship to grow slowly—mentally, emotionally, socially, and spiritually. We would hold hands, talk, laugh, pray, worship, study, and sing funny songs. The occasional kiss kept our relationship transparent and relaxed.

My time with Charlotte was a gift from God. The more I was with her, the more I felt that she was the girl I wanted to marry. I kept that between me and God, however. When the semester was over, Charlotte left for New Mexico and summer school near her home while I prepared for another busy summer selling books. Charlotte told me that at the beginning of the summer she made a major decision not to date anyone while she was at home. This decision certainly gave me more confidence in our relationship, and I was becoming more convinced that I wanted to—and would—marry her. By the end of the summer I was so sure where I stood that I called her on the phone from Delaware, Ohio, and asked her to marry me. She said, "No, I am not ready." But just like the very first time when I asked her to go out with me, what I heard was "Yes, but not now." Amazingly, I was not discouraged.

Our reunion was beyond words back on the Harding campus. When I met her, my heart was leaping out of my chest, pounding with such force that she could feel my heart beating as we embraced.

And so the fall of 1964 was an exciting beginning for me. My summer had been a success, and I had been able to make enough to pay for the following school year. I was chosen to be business manager of *The Bison*, the school newspaper, a position that brought with it a significant stipend to help with expenses. I chose not to run for a class office. Instead I concentrated on my studies and enhanced my relationship with Charlotte.

Of all the memories from that fall, the most significant is a decision that Charlotte made. Sometime before then she had told me that if she ever said, "I love you," it would only be to the person she was willing to marry. One weekend in October I took her over to Memphis to meet my grandmother, Mama Etta. As we got ready to leave town, we sat in the car outside 2181 Washington Street.

Charlotte turned to me and spontaneously said, "I love you."

I did not waste any time. "Will you marry me?" I asked.

"Yes!"

The extra money I saved from my summer work, combined with the money from *The Bison,* allowed us to go ring hunting back in Searcy. By Christmas, we had found a ring in time for the drive to Charlotte's home in New Mexico. I remember going down to the barn where her mother was milking the cows and asking her if I could marry her daughter. Later her mother said that of all the boyfriends Charlotte had over the years, I was her favorite, so much so that she even named one of the cows after me. Charlotte's father, James, was a kind, passive, and gentle man who loved his land and worked it, but he was somewhat disengaged from family members and was hard for me to get to know.

We made many trips back out west over the years, and I never grew tired of watching Charlotte crawl up in her mother's lap and laugh and rest. We were always refreshed whenever we spent time there.

Back at college, Charlotte worked hard in her classes and was planning on being an elementary school teacher while I looked into a military chaplaincy—eventually hoping to serve in Vietnam. The Vietnam War was going strong. I was making plans to enter the chaplaincy to do my part in supporting the young people in the military. I had an internal urge to help others find their way. Part of this urge was the residue of my childhood desire to help Daddy, but I believe part was the call of God on my life. Hungry to learn even more about God, I decided to study theology at graduate school. It would mean learning Hebrew, Greek, and Aramaic plus learning the history of Christianity from the first century till now.

Spring and the early summer of 1965 became our season of preparation for marriage as well as graduation time. Charlotte was chosen as Petit Jean Queen; Petit Jean was the name of the school's yearbook, and one young woman was chosen as queen and featured as an outstanding student. I was selected to receive the Regina Spirit award—a leadership award given to one student in the senior class who represented the Christian Spirit. I didn't know the award existed, and I certainly was not seeking recognition, but I think that perhaps my daily time alone in my room was starting to change me for the better. I was trying to treat others better, so maybe that was why they gave it to me. Whatever the reason, I felt honored.

Reflecting now on the affirmation we both received from classmates and faculty, I think I can see things a little more clearly. During my encounter with the Holy Spirit in the fall of 1963, I experienced a sense that the Holy Spirit was explaining to the Father the feelings I had no language to express. All that desperation I had lived with since seven years old exploded inside me, and in spite of the confusion, I knew that God was there through his Holy Spirit attending to my soul. I felt the Divine Therapist was at work, and that encounter gave me the passion to pray more and study the Scriptures every day.

"I felt the Divine Therapist was at work."

That evening in 1963 changed me and opened my eyes to wonderful writers who became special gifts along with King David in the

Psalms and the writers of Proverbs. Even though academically I was not the brightest bulb on the campus, my heart was full of joy and peace each day. I tried to treat others with respect and compassion that came from an internal awareness that God loved me. Only he could have orchestrated the internal changes that were happening in me. All I did was give him time and a place.

Meanwhile, Charlotte graduated with honors, cum laude. I, on the other hand, just graduated. Thankfully, I had been accepted on probation into Harding University Graduate School of Theology in Memphis. I received a half tuition scholarship, and Charlotte was offered a position as a second grade teacher at Harding Academy. Adjoining the Graduate School were campus apartments where we would live for the next three years.

As the wedding date approached in late summer, I returned to work in Ohio, setting money aside to get us off to a good start. Charlotte spent the summer making her own wedding dress and scraping together money from what little work she could find in New Mexico. Paid summer jobs were nonexistent in Dora, and from the world's point of view, she was poor. All I could see in her was the richest girl I had ever met. She was full of life and free.

To earn what she could, Charlotte cleaned the church building each week and painted for her grandfathers. Grandfather Richards stood over her to make sure she worked fast so he wouldn't have to pay so much, and Grandfather Burkett stood over her to make sure she did a perfect job. But she wasn't flustered. Charlotte has always been secure in herself. She was offered a beautiful wedding dress worn by Beverly, my older brother's wife, but she turned it down, thinking she would have to have a nicer wedding to go with that dress. She decided to make her own dress and have the wedding the way she could afford.

Having sold all the books I had in Ohio, I returned home to Memphis in preparation for the journey west and the wedding. The trouble was that I was as sick as a dog. I had prayed all along that if it was not God's will that I marry Charlotte, he would make it clear to me. Was this illness a sign? Daddy called the doctor, who came to the house and gave me a shot. I recovered, yet not quite enough to drive the thousand miles to join my wife-to-be. So my seventy-three-year-old grandmother, Mama Etta, flew with me to Lubbock, Texas, before driving on to New Mexico.

On August 18, 1965, 2:30 p.m., we were married in the little community church in Dora. It was a simple affair; the ceremony was early in the afternoon so the farmers could get to their afternoon milking. My friend Richard Hughes performed the wedding with Daddy serving as best man. After the reception at the community center, we left late in the afternoon to begin our five-day honeymoon, which we spent taking our time driving across Texas and Arkansas to get to Memphis, Tennessee. Once we got there, Charlotte would begin teaching, and I would start graduate school. If ever in my life I felt as though I were facing a new beginning, this was it.

It is

not you

who shapes

GOD

It is God

who shapes

you.

—Irenaeus

CHAPTER SIX

I Am a Stranger to My Mother

1965–1969

LIFE SEEMED good. During the first three years of our marriage, we lived and loved in a one-bedroom apartment on the campus of Harding in Memphis, Tennessee. Charlotte taught second grade while I stretched my brain in graduate school. I made a little extra money by driving a school bus, and I worked with teenagers on the weekend. Our life was full. It was a happy time.

To get off probation and keep the scholarship, I had to maintain a B average. I was taking classes in Greek, Life Literature, and Thoughts of the Early Church, as well as courses in Christian Education and Counseling. I felt so inadequate in this academic setting. The only way I would be able to accomplish what was being asked of me was to have God's help. Each and every day I was driven to prayer, relying on God for the help I needed to get through the daily challenges. I was very thankful for the ability to work hard at my studies, and I got the results I needed. I even managed to grab a few As over the course of three years.

Windows of learning were opening to me, and I loved the inspiration I drew from my fellow students. Meanwhile, working with the teenagers on the weekend kept my feet on the ground, helping to make sure I did not get too lost in the world of academic theory. God's story is profound and intriguing and worthy of study and discourse by the brightest people among us, but theologians sure don't have a monopoly on understanding God. God's story relates to the greatest and the least among us, including me.

"God's story relates to the greatest and the least among us, including me."

Life for a young married couple before they have children usually is a lot simpler. Charlotte had eight students in her class and made $4,000 a year. I made $10 a week working with teens, which paid for our food each week. The little I made driving the school bus twice a day helped us meet our other weekly expenses. We were able to dedicate ourselves to making the best start that we could of this journey together.

During the first summer, we worked as youth counselors at a Christian camp. I was the lifeguard at the large pond where the kids swam. I had told them not to go in the water until I arrived because of the poisonous snakes that might be in the water. One day, I arrived at swim time and found a young boy already in the water by himself. I gave him a pretty strong telling off and made him get out of the water and come up on the bank. As he pulled himself out of the water, I saw that he had just one leg. He wanted to get in the water before the others so nobody would see that he was missing a leg. Now I had made his self-consciousness so much worse. I felt awful, but it was the first time in my life I was thankful for my legs.

Throughout the summer, to fill in for a friend, I did a fifteen-minute radio program and then spoke at a community church over in Pontotoc, Mississippi. I did a lot of oral interpretive readings of the Psalms and the Gospels since my major in undergraduate school was communication. This was yet another challenging and positive new experience.

It was inevitable that at some point Charlotte and I would hit rockier ground. And we did. The cause was my desire to go into the military as a chaplain. Even though I investigated the possibilities on my own, somehow I never communicated this hope to Charlotte. It seems odd now, but that is the truth. After I completed the Master of Theology, we spent the summer in Houston, Texas, while I worked as a chaplain's intern at M. D. Anderson Medical Center. I learned so much that summer, including the fact that I was wholly uncomfortable with the notion of death. My supervisor made that perfectly clear to me one day. He observed me as I spoke with a man who was dying. As the man began to describe his feelings regarding his death, I changed the subject to the baseball game being played that evening. It was not a deliberate or conscious decision on my part, but my supervisor noticed and called it to my attention. I realized that I simply did not want to face death.

The idea of a military chaplaincy concerned Charlotte. She was worried that I would spend too much time away from her and our future family. This was not what she had envisioned for our marriage. It had been my dream for years, and the idea of giving it up felt like a mighty difficult hurdle to overcome. But when we discovered that Charlotte was pregnant with our first child, my view of the future changed quickly. Not only did I not want to put Charlotte through the trials of bringing up a child with a frequently absent father, I no longer wanted to leave. I wanted my future to be wherever Charlotte was. Besides, as my supervisor pointed out, I might not be ideally suited to the job after all.

So, as the new life grew inside Charlotte, I searched out different possibilities for our future. The Memphis church where I had been working with youth all the way through graduate school hired me for an interim period. They asked me to help lead their educational program and continue to work with the youth, which I did with pleasure.

Those were strange days. Not only was the war in Vietnam at its peak in 1968, but the civil rights movement was challenging all of our perceptions about race. I had grown up in the South and had seen segregation in force all my life. It seemed unremarkable that a restaurant had four restrooms—two for black people and two for whites—and the fact that black families could visit the Memphis zoo only one day a week was just another example of how life had always been.

Although I was raised in a racially segregated southern culture, I was already on the road to being transformed into seeing people as just people, not separated by divisions of race. I had been actively involved in an African American church during my undergraduate days, and I was well acquainted with the first black students who were admitted to Harding's campus in Searcy. I knew that Christ knew no color: all people were made in the image of God.

Everything seemed to be changing in our society. Our ideas

about what was right and wrong—and what could be made different—were shifting. Old lessons were being unlearned, and new ideas were being explored. Then in the spring of 1968—three miles from Frank Street in Memphis, Tennessee—Martin Luther King Jr. was assassinated. We were in Memphis at the graduate school, living on campus. Dr. King had been in the city to lead a march on behalf of the sanitation workers. He gave his famous "I've been to the mountaintop" speech downtown on the evening of April 3 and was shot the next day outside his motel room.

Right away, a citywide curfew was put in place. We watched the news with images of riots taking place all over the country, and not surprisingly, word got around that there was trouble in Memphis. We got together with a few of the other married couples and ate our meals in front of the TV, glued to it for all we were worth. For many people in the city, Dr. King was nothing more than a troublemaker, but for us, he was a man whose life had been cruelly ended before he could complete his good work. It felt as though life itself was tearing apart, and we started to pray for peace and hope.

But the troubles came even closer to home. I experienced personal grief too deeply and too frequently that year. First was the sudden death of Dr. Paul Rotenberry, one of my professors at the graduate school. He was a gracious and gifted teacher, and his death shocked us all. Yet out of the grief came a moment of clarity that encouraged me. I was with a friend who knew Dr. Rotenberry better than I had. My friend was struggling not just with the sadness but with faith itself. He was stricken with the knowledge that he would never have the opportunity to talk with Dr. Rotenberry again.

"Terry, there are two or three questions I wish I could have asked him," lamented my friend.

"You know what he would have said," I replied, "because you were with him. You drank coffee with him after class; he would ride around in your sports car with you; you had dinner in his home. No student knew him better than you. You knew how he thought."

My friend looked at me with a smile of sudden realization. "Yes," he said, "that's right. I did. Thank you."

"We ought to know the mind of Christ so well that at any fork in the road, we would know his response."

I said to him, "We ought to know the mind of Christ so well that at any fork in the road, we would know his response."

He looked at me, and I looked at him, and we both knew our eyes had been opened. We did not share our questions with each other at the time, but that conversation turned out to be a marker moment for both of us. My direction was set. I could think of no compass greater than following what mattered to Christ. These many years later, I have yet to change my mind.

My friend eventually told me about his intellectual questions and how our interchange that day had driven him to pursue a Ph.D. in higher criticism. His path ended up in academia. He found the answers he sought and went on to teach and equip seminary students for lives of ministry. My questions were relational, and my path would lead into the depths of broken marriages, broken families, and broken lives, specifically the life of my broken mother.

Another death that year struck close to home and was even more painful. Martha had written me a beautiful note of friendship and affirmation right before Charlotte and I married. Martha's relationship to me had been long, starting back when we were barely teenagers. It ended when we turned twenty-one, but she remained a very important person in my life.

August 9, 1965

Dear Terry—

Just saw your wedding announcement in the Clarksdale paper, and I wanted to tell you how much I wish you all the happiness and success in the world. For so many years you have meant so much to me—and I hope that this special feeling can now be translated into friendship. I have only happiest memories of our association, and I shall always cherish them.

I realize what a wonderfully important and exciting time of your life this is—and I just wanted you to know that I'm thinking about you now and wishing for you all the good things of life—and—above all—the blessing of God in whatever you do!

Love, Martha

Life had not been easy for her. Growing up, I found that hard to believe, what with her family's wealth and status. But you never know what goes on behind closed doors, and her father's suicide in the fall of 1962 showed just how far from perfect their life was.

Having tried, but failed, to comfort her after her father's death, I made contact with her once more while I was at graduate school in Memphis. I just wanted to know she was doing well, and we talked on the phone for a short time. As always, she was very gracious.

In December 1968 my sister called to tell me that Martha died. Tragically, she killed herself with the same gun her father used to take his life. This loss cut deeply into my soul. Why did she do it? What happened to bring her to such a desperate point in her life? Could I have done anything? So many unanswered questions existed. They still do. What happens in the recesses of the soul to cause such pain and loss? I wanted to know, and in time I would begin to understand a little of what drives and shapes us. I have become familiar with grief, and I know a little better the ways in which the death of a loved one can affect people. But not then. As a wide-eyed twenty-something, I was put into a spin. Grief hurt and left me feeling overwhelmed.

"Grief hurt and left me feeling overwhelmed."

With the assassination of Dr. King, the sudden death of Dr. Rotenberry, and Martha's suicide, I was forced to deal with the reality of death in more than an intellectual way. In addition to personal losses, my choice of career put me in a place of dealing constantly with death, both physical and relational, and I needed answers. Focusing on the mind of Christ was the path that I was choosing—how he dealt with people, with failure, with pain. I wondered whether God could really help someone like Mama. Could he salvage a soul so wounded by the storms of life? Could he handle something that big, something that messed up? Someone whose life was shattered beyond recognition? These questions drove me.

All that year, I had been driving the school bus by where Mama was living. Twice a day, every day, I looked for her. *I had not seen Mama in eighteen years*. My stomach contracted and left me feeling nauseous as I tried to get a glimpse of her as I passed her house.

Strangely, I never saw her. Much of the time as I drove by, I did not mind that she never appeared. I knew Daddy hated her, and my feelings about her were deeply conflicted. So just looking at a permanently closed door from behind the glass suited me fine.

As for the rest of the family, Sid spent two years in the army and now worked for the IRS in Washington, DC. Robert graduated from high school in 1966. Carol was married with a son and a daughter. Daddy and my stepmom and their daughter, Patricia, lived in Clarksdale.

Finishing my degree at Harding School of Theology, I had a summer internship at M. D. Anderson in Houston, Texas, and then returned to Memphis. I had been invited to stay in the little Memphis church where I earlier had worked with their young people. This gave us a place to live as well as some work while we waited to see what would open next for us. I began to think about Mama in new ways, perhaps just because once again I was back in Memphis. Perhaps it was because our own family was growing, but whatever the reason, I decided it was time to pay Mama a proper visit.

I was twenty-six years old—young enough to still feel like her child, but old enough to know that I could not just knock on her door out of mere curiosity. I had to be willing to get to know her. I had to be willing to risk getting hurt again. I wanted to find out what God might do. So, with Charlotte at my side, I knocked. An elderly man came to the door. I told him that I wanted to see Mildred, and he asked who I was.

"Tell her it is her son. I am Mildred's son."

Soon, she came to the door. She looked smaller and older but still young. She looked at me, scanning my face for clues. "Robert?" she asked.

"No. I'm not Robert. It's me, Bubba."

She opened the screen door and invited us in. We sat in the living room and talked. There were no bottles around so I assumed that if she was still drinking, this was one of her sober periods.

She was pleasant and happy to meet her new daughter-in-law

and hear about her future grandchild being on the way. It felt right to be there. I realized I had been feeling incomplete inside, plagued by too many unanswered questions about her story and mine, and bothered by the volume of things that I did not know. I wanted to hear her side of the story, and all my training as a counselor taught me how to listen. It also taught me that I needed to do more than just meet up with her once, get some answers, tell her about Jesus, and then leave. If I wanted it to count, I had to see this as the beginning of a journey that would take years.

"I had to see this as the beginning of a journey that would take years."

That first meeting was brief, but I was encouraged. Even though I had no idea what I was doing, I kept thinking she was the woman Jesus had met at the well in Samaria—a woman who had had five husbands and who was living with a man who was not her husband. The facts of Mama's life were similar. At that point she had gone through five divorces, and the man who answered the door was not her husband.

Jesus never shied away from people scarred by their mistakes. Instead, he faced them with *love and honesty,* offering challenge and acceptance in equal measure. Would that work for Mama? Did this "Jesus thinking" work in real life? Would his words be the key to bring living water to Mama in the same way that they brought living water to the woman at the well? I knew Jesus was the only One who made any sense for a broken and empty life like that of Mama, and I was desperate to see that it was true.

After our first meeting, I invited her to hear me speak one Sunday evening. When she finally did, it was the first time she had been in a church building in seventeen or eighteen years. The message I presented was an oral reading of the entire Sermon on the Mount in the Revised Standard Version. She listened and said, "This is the first sermon I ever understood." But we never talked about it afterward. It was awkward for her. How could it not have been?

Many questions rose within me during this year. The assassination of a good man, the brokenness of a woman who failed her family, the suicide of a dear friend, and the sudden, untimely death of my teacher—all left me desperate for answers like a drowning man gasping for air. And yet the search for answers was paying off. I did not drown. I found the question behind all the other questions, the one true thing that I needed to ask in order to make sense of all this chaos and loss. My question was simple: Do the lessons Christ taught work in real life with people as broken as Mama?

"Jesus never shied away from people scarred by their mistakes."

PART THREE

You don't get to make up most of your story.
You get to make peace with it.

You don't get to demand your life, like a given.
You get to accept your life, like a gift.

Beginnings and middles, they are only yours to embrace,
to unwrap like a gift.

But you get the endings. You *always* get the endings.
You get the endings and you get to make them
a gift back to the Giver.

—*Ann Voskamp*

CHAPTER SEVEN

I Am Dangerous

1969–1979

PEOPLE RECOILED when they first saw Bob Nelson. His face was disfigured, not just by the horrific burns he endured as a child but by the countless surgeries that scarred him in the years that followed. But once you had taken in the failings of his skin that stretched and creased over his body like a makeshift patchwork, it was almost impossible not to feel completely at ease with Bob. He was comfortable with himself, and he was comfortable with others. He was both the rebel and the wounded, and we became good friends.

I met him when he arrived at the University of Memphis. It was 1969, and I had taken a position as director of the Christian Student Center on campus. Bob had an older sister, Martha, who had gone to Harding with me in the early 1960s. Their mother brought him over to the Student Center to meet me. Bob was a brilliant student and about to graduate with honors from undergraduate school in business. Despite what his mother thought, he really had no time for a campus minister like me. We had a short conversation about inconsequential things, and then he left.

Several months after our introduction, he returned to see me. He had an application for work at an outstanding real estate company and was struggling to complete part of the form. There, next to the box marked "Friends" there was only blank space.

"I don't have any friends," he said, "just drinking buddies."

I took my pen out of my pocket and pitched it to him. I said, "You can put down my name."

And so began a deep friendship that lasted until his early death.

Bob's story starts when he was two years old, playing with his older brother outside. There was a bonfire, and his brother handed him a bottle of what he thought was water to throw on the fire. But there was no water in the bottle; it was white kerosene.

The flames that reached for Bob's clothes and skin left him severely burned. Over the next fifteen years he had seventeen plastic surgeries, spending more time in the hospital than he spent away from it. His best friend was his plastic surgeon, but when Bob was seventeen, the surgeon was killed in a car accident. Bob became a rebel, a strong-willed and ever-questioning skeptic. He rejected the superficial religious explanations that were laid out before him, seeing them as futile and fake attempts to address the tragedy of his life and the larger problems in the world.

I was unable to answer his questions, although I could understand why he chose to reject religious exclusivity and choose personal rebellion instead. Our backgrounds were completely different. His parents were deeply loving of him and each other, as well as being religious, while mine did not know how to love themselves, their children, or God. But Bob's most pressing question—"Where is God in the midst of injustice and death?"—glowed brightly within me as well. If there was one difference between us in this respect, it was that I was just a few years ahead of him in searching for the answer.

At the age of twenty-four, Bob went through his next great personal health crisis. He was told that the vein under his heart was clogged and needed to be replaced with a synthetic one. If not, he would be dead within two months. Yet there were risks to the surgery, and they gave him just a one in ten chance of making it through the operation.

They operated in the spring of 1974. Bob made it through, but he remained critical as his recovery failed to take root. His brain began to swell, and the staff feared that the damage it caused might be permanent. The doctors scrawled "no heroics" on his chart, instructing all staff not to resuscitate him if he slipped into a coma.

Six months later, I was standing with Bob at a seminar, interviewing him about his health experience in front of the students. His miraculous recovery was truly inspirational, and it occurred to me that he would be the perfect intern to take on in a new project that was being set up at Harding in Searcy. A nursing program was being established on campus, and I could think of nobody better qualified to help train the nursing students on how to be sensitive to dying patients. Besides, Bob was training me how to be with people in emotional and physical pain. Bob was ten years younger than I, but I felt like he was ten years older.

Bob had grown up in a nurturing family, and he knew so much more than I did about how to love. I asked him if he would guard my back and tell me if he saw me not being attentive to Charlotte or my children the way a husband and father should be. I gave him permission to correct me and to talk with Charlotte privately to check on how she was experiencing me.

Our friendship continued to blossom as his health continued to deteriorate. The synthetic vein stopped working, and the doctors could offer no explanation for why he was still living. A beautiful lady that he met at the University of Memphis loved him and wanted to marry him. Bob loved her, but he knew that he did not have much time left. His compassion and care for her were greater than his desire to have her with him as he faced death, so he deliberately broke off the relationship. I have never known a greater love story.

One day, he and I were traveling together, discussing Scripture.

"Terry, do you know the psalm that says, 'Teach us to number our days, that we may gain a heart of wisdom'?"

I told him that I did know that psalm.

"Well, I number my days by one," he said.

And then he was gone four years later. He died while he was at home with his mom and dad. Thirty years of physical suffering and no opportunity to live out his dreams to find a wife and raise a family. That was Bob's lot, and it seemed like injustice. Who speaks to this real-life dilemma? Bob can speak for himself. On the eve of his surgery to insert a synthetic vein in his heart years earlier, he said these words to me: "If I live, praise God! If I die, praise God! I trust the God who loved me enough to give his only Son to die for me!"

"Bob knew that God is a God of love, that he is larger than death."

Bob's spiritual quest was larger than the religious

beliefs that were handed to him. Bob knew that God is a God of love, that he is larger than death. Bob knew his story was not over. I asked Bob if he had learned anything he could share with us. He said that the most important lesson he learned was how to get dressed inside each day. I asked him what he meant, and he referred to the letter written by Paul to the Ephesians, which describes the process of putting on the spiritual armor of God. It was an internal action, a matter of the soul. I realized that what Bob said was right. Even though much in my life was significantly better than it had been, I still carried around within me a soul wound with hidden toxic beliefs. Every day, they threatened to sabotage not only me but also those around me. I did not have the leisure to skip a day getting dressed spiritually in the morning; I would be too disabled to function.

"The most important lesson he learned was how to get dressed inside each day."

Bob's story had intertwined with mine when I was at the University of Memphis and continued afterward. It was a period when I established many deep and lasting friendships. It was also a time when I became eager to share the joy of God's love and to lead students to know and share it for themselves. I woke up early each morning to spend time with God and hung out late at night, meeting students in the dorms, sharing the things I was learning. Soon I realized I could share only the things God actually taught me. If there was one lesson I learned better than others, it was that true success depended on the answer to this simple question: Have I let Jesus be Lord of my life today?

With that as my compass, I found myself drawn into all types of adventures during these years of campus work. I met a man named David Wade, who was waiting for a kidney transplant but needed daily treatment. This could be given only through a dialysis machine, and there was only one in Memphis then. David was not a part of our group but a member of another tribe of Christians. Regardless of his background, our students decided to help. General Mills, Inc., challenged people to collect 600,000 Betty Crocker coupons in return for which the company would donate a kidney machine. A small group formed with Bob Nelson as a key player. Despite so many people saying that the target was unreachable, God answered their prayer. Within three months they collected 1.6 million coupons and put $18,000 in the bank for David's treatment. They also persuaded the mayor of Memphis to get involved. In the end, eighteen new kidney machines were donated to area hospitals. They even managed to get a law enacted in the state of Tennessee that placed the choice to be an organ donor on every driver's license. It was clearly a work of God that David's life was saved. No matter that David was not part of our group; he was a person in our path who needed help. And we upheld Jesus' urging to love one's neighbor.

Unfortunately, this desire to help people outside the tribe got me into trouble. Some of the church leaders became critical of the work I was doing, accusing me of being a liberal. That accusation stung. *Liberal* was the equivalent of a four-letter word in my tribe, and labeling me as one was a serious charge.

My youth, my passion to share the love of Christ, and my immaturity left some religious leaders mistrustful of my work on the campus. Many folks viewed my work as a success, but the old guard leaders did not know quite what to do with me. I did not know what to do with me either, other than rise every day and pray that I would be faithful to love as Jesus loved. Every day, God was changing me, but at the same time, I felt that I was about to be abandoned.

"I did not know what to do with me either, other than rise every day and pray that I would be faithful to love as Jesus loved."

Not having had a spiritually focused mother or father, I discovered a secret place where I could go for help. There, I found language for the pain I was feeling. I found promises that gave me hope. I found a world that spoke of an unseen joy. I found honest anger and deep depression processed in the open in poetic language. I found a way to orient my disoriented soul. When Jesus quoted the psalmist as he hung on the cross—"My God, my God, why have you forsaken me?"—I found a man who spoke about a God who "is near to the brokenhearted and saves those who are crushed in spirit." Reading Proverbs was like sitting down with a good father who spoke plainly about wisdom, money, sex, and power.

I needed plenty of counsel. Landon Saunders was a bit older than I, and he had become nationally prominent as a

"I needed plenty of counsel."

visionary speaker. I had invited Landon to speak at one of our university conferences. A student asked him, "What do you do in the mornings?" and he shared that he read five chapters of Psalms and one chapter of Proverbs every morning. From that point I started the same practice of working through each book once a month. Truly, Psalms was becoming my mother and Proverbs my father.

I needed the help, particularly when our student group encountered a major racial issue. One of my responsibilities was taking students to visit the churches in the city that were financially supporting our work on campus. I delivered a program that involved reading Scripture, praying, singing, and providing a speaker to tell the story of the vision we had on campus. This approach worked well, keeping people informed and giving the students the opportunity to exercise new gifts.

The week I planned the campus presentation for my home congregation, I decided to include several young people who were leaders in our campus group. I took an outline of the participants to my home church—a large church with a congregation of eight or nine hundred people—to have it printed. Later, I got a call saying an elder had seen the program and had concerns about one young man—an African American—reading the Scripture. I visited with the overseeing elder and told him I would not take the young man off the program.

A crisis developed, and a meeting was called. The elders refused to allow the student to read in church. I told them I wanted them to tell him to his face, and they called him in and did so. He challenged them, but still they refused to back down. He never returned to the church or to our student group. I asked them this question at the end of the meeting: "If a student makes a decision to follow Christ on the university campus, will he be accepted as a member in full fellowship with this church?"

I was livid, and many leaders were upset that I put them in such a difficult spot. Another meeting followed, this time with the deacons who served under the elders, to discuss the situation. I was accused of insubordination, of putting this man on the program to deliberately cause trouble. Searching the book of Proverbs for wisdom, I decided the best thing to do would be to ignore my anger and choose silence as my defense. I watched the Spirit of God work in that meeting of forty or fifty men—some getting angry and resigning, but many more agreeing to create and sign a document that stated any baptized believer who wanted to be a part of this community would be fully accepted as a member, regardless of race.

I am not sure this decision was a complete victory. It was the right thing to do, but it deepened their mistrust of me, and I was saddened that there needed to be a written document in a church to affirm what Christ had already made clear. The mistrust quietly built after this incident until it was clear three years later that I needed to resign.

In addition to Bob Nelson, other great friendships were building: mentors like E. H. Ijams who was in his eighties, Harold Hazelip (dean of the graduate school and preaching minister of the church we attended), Landon Saunders (president and founder of Heartbeat, a nonprofit educational media group), Jim Woodroof (minister, mentor, and author), Carroll Osburn (professor of New Testament Greek at Harding, Pepperdine, and Abilene Christian University), and Bill Lynn and his wife, Sherrill.

Bill and Sherrill had six biological children of their own and adopted two others, but they treated us like family, providing much-needed love and nurture. I introduced Sherrill to Mama, and her family brought Mama into their home to help her overcome her alcoholism and begin a new life. In a true sense, Sherrill became my mother in the faith, and Bill was a dear brother whom I grew to love. All of their children were like my adopted brothers and sisters. It was just like being back with the Roseberrys.

One person to whom I dedicated this book is Liz LaVelle. Liz died at the age of nineteen in a car accident while traveling back to Lipscomb University in the summer of 2010. She was the daughter of Dr. David and Jenny LaVelle and sister to Kate and Dan LaVelle. Liz was the precious granddaughter of Mama Sherrill, my mother in the faith. I was given the same challenge to speak at her memorial service as I was asked by Ty and Nancy Osman to speak words of comfort at the memorial service of Ty II. There are still no words to express the grief and loss of this beautiful life that was dedicated to caring for foster children and giving to others. I called David and Jenny to minister to me as I attempted to stand again in the place to offer hope in a moment of devastating tragedy. I still have no words.

Other friends gathered weekly to pray. Rusty Bloodworth, Mike McGraw, Norma Gelman, Carolyn Moore, Sandy Gates, David Gribble, Becky Mayer, Dan Askew, and Bob Nelson were just a few of them. Rusty had just returned from a fellowship in Scandinavia after receiving his undergraduate degree at the University of Virginia. He was well read on the religions of the world and philosophy. A few weeks before leaving for the States, Rusty had purchased a small New Testament and read it through in one sitting. The impact was life changing and set him on an entirely new course. He arrived in Memphis with a clear belief that Jesus Christ was who he said he was and that he was worth following. Rusty's faith would become a source of inspiration and strength for me over the years. At times, all of these wonderful young people would have all-night prayer sessions at our house, and we saw so many people responding to the joy of God's love. I preached Christ crucified and raised from the dead, staying away from technical church doctrines. In other words I focused on the most basic truths of the faith.

But I was getting the reputation among some of the religious leaders in town of not being a sound teacher of the Word of God. During the 1970s, the whole world was being shaken up like a snow globe. The way cultures were settling meant that the old ways of doing things simply did not make much sense anymore. The Jesus movement was in full bloom, and converted hippies were traveling around to college campuses. There was talk about the end of the world and the urgent need for repentance. I struggled with some of these aspects of their message because it seemed to contradict so much of what Paul preached and what Jesus emphasized. I knew I could teach only what God taught me, and that was a message of love.

"I knew I could teach only what God taught me, and that was a message of love."

Sara Anne was born February 4, 1969, and Kathryn Melissa was born July 5, 1970. Their arrivals brought great joy to our marriage. However, the discovery that great joy and great sorrow could come at the same time was a new experience for me.

In February 1972, we faced a crisis when Charlotte's mother

died suddenly of a heart attack. We left as soon as we heard, driving to New Mexico to be with Charlotte's family. Charlotte was devastated. She had been so close to her mother, who was only sixty-one years old. It was the first time Charlotte had known such grief. She still had all four grandparents, and we had been with her mother and father for Christmas just two months before. The shock was tremendous because her mother seemed fine then.

In addition to the shock, her mother died during the weekend of a seminar I organized on campus, and 1,500 college students planned to attend. I had invited two speakers from outside our church tribe to take part in the seminar, and the church leaders were not happy. Charlotte and I left for New Mexico on the first night, which meant that I would not be around to answer their concerns. Yet again, the accusation of being a liberal was leveled at me, and the tension between me and the leaders continued to grow.

The paternal grandmother, Etta Rutland Smith Stewart.

Mildred and Sidney Smith, Terry's parents (1944).

Terry's third grade class in Clarksdale (1950); Terry is on the far left.

Terry (far right) with his three siblings and mother (1951).

Little League team. Terry is third from the right on first row (1952).

Ina Roseberry Reed.

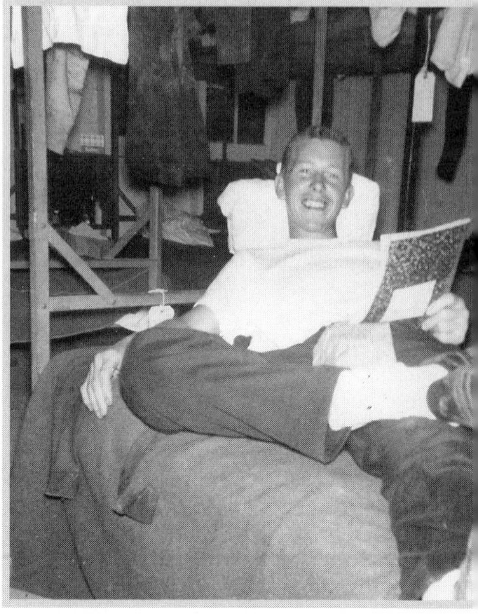

Relaxing in the bunk house after working in the pea fields (1961).

Tennis team at Harding (1965); Terry is second from right, first row.

▲ *Charlotte Burkett, her first year at Harding (1964).*

►*Margy with Bob Nelson (1975).*

Mama Sherrill, Terry's mother in the faith, and Terry.

Liz LaVelle, June 19, 1991 to July 28, 2010.

Ty Osman II, August 27, 1993 to March 4, 2012.

Landon Saunders, spiritual mentor.

Jim and Louine Woodroof.

Rusty and Fran Bloodworth, Jerusalem (2012).

Charlotte, Terry, and Norma Sarvis, Jerusalem (2012).

Family reunion (1990), the first time in 39 years that Terry's parents were in the same place. His father, Sid, and Sid's wife, Jean, are far left. Terry's mother, Mildred, is in the middle of the back row.

The Smith children: Elizabeth, Margaret (Margy), Melissa, and Sara (2002).

Terry and Charlotte with the children and grandchildren, Thanksgiving (2012).

CHAPTER EIGHT

I Can Feel the Flames

1969–1979

THE GUILT and shame Mama felt over her adultery with Daddy's best friend, as well as her inability to forgive herself, and Daddy's refusal to forgive her had been powerful enough to lead her to having a nervous breakdown and making many bad decisions involving men. The elderly man she was living with when I found her had rescued her from her fifth husband—a man who lived in a shack with a dirt floor in south Memphis near the Mississippi border. Her fifth husband had beaten her so badly that most of her bones were broken, and she had been his slave, not caring whether she lived or died. The elderly gentleman and his wife had befriended her in those broken years between husbands. After his wife died, he became Mama's caretaker, and later her sixth husband, until he died.

Throughout this twenty-year period, she medicated with alcohol. She remained stuck in adolescence in 1968, behaving on the emotional level of a sixteen-year-old. Chronologically, she was forty-five years old, but her head and heart were those of a child. Her emotional and spiritual growth stopped, and I was embarking on an unknown path with the hope that we could make a difference in her life. This decision to include her in my life unfortunately separated me from Daddy because his hate for her consumed him. He could not speak her name to me or share anything about what had happened in the breakup of the family. But now, for the first time, I began to hear her early family background from her point of view and what her world was like during those early married years with Daddy.

Perhaps that was why some of the students with whom I was working took her into their group and gave her love and support. Perhaps they were experiencing her more as a wounded peer than a parent figure. Much later Mama Sherrill told me that she could see that Mama planned to break up my marriage so she could reclaim her son. Like the teenager she was inside, Mama was demanding more and more of my attention. I found myself sacrificing the care of my family to meet her demands. But I felt that I should save her.

"I found myself sacrificing the care of my family to meet her demands."

The breakthrough began one evening when Mama called me, and she was drunk. The ringing phone woke the children and robbed me of a night's sleep. When we spoke about it the next day, she could not remember the conversation. This began to happen more frequently until I answered one midnight call with the words: "Don't ever call me again when you are drinking. I will not talk to you."

She was shocked and never called drunk again. Later she told me: "That was the first time I realized that I really wanted to live."

It was the beginning of my long journey with her as she made her first faltering steps toward life. Mama was coming from a place where she hated herself; she despised her very existence. She experienced failure after failure in marriage and life. She abandoned her four children and was on a path to certain death. Every holiday, every birthday had found Mama miserable and suicidal. But now she was making a decision to live, and I wanted to walk beside her all the way.

I was anxious and unconsciously wanted to rush her progress. I was overeager to affirm Mama, wanting my children to have a relationship with their grandmother. During the summer of 1971, I planned a weekend retreat for the college students and wanted Charlotte to let Mama take care of the children while Charlotte and I went on the retreat. One afternoon after I had suggested this arrangement, I got a call at work from Charlotte.

"I am leaving you," she said.

I told her I would be right home. On arrival, I found my aunt Myrtle and uncle Ernest there to take Charlotte and the children to their house. We talked, and I became acutely aware that my plan to turn over our two-and-a-half-year-old and our eleven-month-old to my alcoholic mother was not going to happen on her watch. I know now that it takes a heavy drinker at least a year to get mentally clear. I was ignorant of this reality then, but Charlotte was courageous and drew the line in the right place, even though I was not listening. As she explained, I finally understood how slow I had been to grasp the truth of her concerns.

I did not make this mistake again, and the incident led to an improvement in things between Charlotte and me. The tension between Charlotte and me was there because we were ill equipped to talk through difficult issues. Neither of our families modeled good communication skills in dealing with conflict. But Charlotte asked for two things that proved to be life changing for our family: first, that I be at home for evening dinner, and second, that I be around to help put the children to bed. My chaotic upbringing and lack of boundaries as a child left me with a huge blind spot. I might have been well intentioned, but I was ignorant of the children's needs. Charlotte's requests became a wonderful gift to me as well as to the children.

Meanwhile, I was becoming increasingly aware of my weaknesses and failures at work. The students were my best teachers, but I am aware today of how I mishandled so many of their lives. I know I gave them my best, but one's best, offered in ignorance, often causes damage. One story from this time stands out more than all the others.

Ellen was a freshman at the university, and she lived in a dorm on campus. One evening several students, including Ellen, and I gathered for a discussion group, and I shared that the key to life was spiritual. Ellen reacted with overt hostility, saying that God was not relevant to her. She went on a verbal rampage, questioning how God could allow all the evil to exist in the world. My response was short but kind. I said that I did not recognize the God she was talking about. When I ran into her on campus the following day, she apologized profusely for how rudely she treated me.

That was the start of what would become a strong friendship over the years between Ellen, Charlotte, our daughters Sara, Missy, Margy, Elizabeth, and me. Her father was a lawyer and a closet alcoholic, and she had grown up overhearing his abuse of her mother night after night. Ellen became her mother's confidante and counselor early in her life. She learned to please people who showed her love.

Though Ellen continued to remain skeptical about religious faith, I pushed her hard to join us for a spiritual retreat. She finally agreed, and it was a very positive weekend. Ellen and I walked and talked together. Our friendship had grown, and she made a decision over the weekend to make a spiritual commitment of faith. She was no longer the great skeptic; she was now a believer. Ellen became a leader in the student group, and many people trusted her advice. It was amazing to watch the sudden change from skeptic to advocate.

This is where I failed Ellen. The process of coming to faith is often difficult—a journey that needs to be fully traveled without shortcuts. Ellen was responding more to her need to please us rather than working through many of her legitimate questions and coming to faith in that way.

Ellen met a young man who was taking one of my classes at the university, and they hit it off well. After several months he proposed marriage. Bob was intelligent, handsome, and had a promising future. He came from a good family, and everyone, especially Ellen's mother, was pleased with this new couple. We thought the young man was wonderful, and from all we could see, it was a great match.

As their premarital counselor I failed to see the reality of what was happening. Just as it had been with her faith, so it was with her marriage. She had a lot of doubts, but she did not express them. She married Bob because she thought the marriage would please her mom, and she wanted to please us. Unfortunately, the marriage ended twelve years later.

My failure goes back to my eagerness for her to move from the dark place I saw in her life to the brightness of good relationships. I wanted her to move quickly, yet she needed to go more slowly. She needed to understand that we are not loved because we get everything right; we are loved because of God's goodness and grace.

"She needed to understand that we are not loved because we get everything right; we are loved because of God's goodness and grace."

Ellen's concept of God was rooted in the way her father treated her mother. She had only two choices: rage against him or quietly obey in fear. Because I did not understand this or grasp my unhealthy eagerness to help her on her journey, Charlotte and I lost two good friends. Thankfully, Ellen eventually found the freedom to search out her own life without my unintentional smothering.

At thirty, I was just beginning to discover my toxicity. It was a strange element in my character, and I had a hard time seeing it. My sense of being responsible for people was overdeveloped, and yet this unconscious belief system was not something I understood. I could not see the seriousness of my problem. To believe in someone means you treat her with respect; you do not treat her as if she is incapable of thinking through her own life, but this is exactly what I was doing. This deep-seated tendency toward overresponsibility has been one of the major obstacles in my life, and it also hindered others from being their best selves. What I thought was my greatest strength was turning out to be one of my greatest weaknesses. While I thought I was helping and caring for others, I was in fact struggling under an unconscious need to succeed by saving them. It was my Messiah Complex.

During the fall of 1970, I met James Woodroof, a minister who returned to Memphis after five years as a missionary in New Zealand. Jim filled in for me from time to time, teaching my Biblical Studies course at the university when I was unable to teach. We developed a friendship that extended to the tennis court. He soon left Memphis to assume the post of senior minister for students at my old alma mater, Harding. I was invited to Harding to speak at a conference in the fall of 1973, and Jim told me that he wanted me to join him in his work. I felt there was no way I could return to a Christian school. My work was directed toward university students who were not in a Christian school. With so many Christians at a Christian college, how could I be of any use?

A few months passed. On the morning of Tuesday, December 18, 1973, I went to the University of Memphis campus to meet with any students who wanted to gather for contemplation and prayer. I felt compelled to go to my office, kneel down, and pray. I saw a puzzle as I prayed, and the puzzle was my work in Memphis. It seemed the last piece of the puzzle was being put in the picture. Immediately, it became clear to me that my work at this place was done. I didn't know all the reasons why, but I trusted my senses. In January of that same year, I had sought counsel from Dr. E. H. Ijams, a wise teacher and former president of Lipscomb University. I told him what had been happening and concluded my remarks with the statement, "The bottom line is, I think the elder board is going to fire me."

With a twinkle in his eye, his response was clear: "I think you are right!"

The Lynn family had become an important part of our lives in Memphis and was greatly involved in our campus work. Due to personal conflicts, the leadership at my church had become critical of the Lynn family and their involvement with the students. The Lynns were helping us reach out to students who were trying to leave the culture of illicit drugs so prevalent in the early 1970s. Their home was a safe place for broken students as well as my mother, for whom Mama Sherrill cared so graciously as she healed from alcohol abuse. As the church leadership became critical, I became critical. Things were coming to a head.

I had tested the ministry's Board of Elders earlier in May, meeting with them and asking if they wanted me to continue my work on campus. Surprisingly, they gave me a unanimous "Yes." Even then, I did not feel they were shooting straight with me, but I took them at their word and stayed. Now in December, I knew it was time to leave. I rose from my knees, went next door to my associate, Ben Williams, and told him that I was resigning. It was the end of the semester, and I had completed most of my courses. Basically, I was done.

"My interpretation of this moment was that God was prompting me to act."

Then I went home to tell Charlotte. Unfortunately, she was less convinced. She couldn't see how I could resign in the middle of a year, but I disagreed. My interpretation of this moment was that God was prompting me to act. Charlotte agreed to pray for a sign, and the next morning I wrote my letter of resignation on a napkin while eating breakfast at a restaurant.

That evening I was called in with Ben to meet with an elder who oversaw my campus work. He made it clear that if I ever tried to run any aspect of the campus work without the direct oversight and approval of the elders, he would not hesitate to ask for my resignation. In some ways I was shocked. I had been working with others throughout my four and a half years at Memphis, so why raise it as an issue now? But greater than the sense of surprise, I felt reassured and relieved: here was the sign that Charlotte and I were looking for. They had been accusing me of being a liberal for a while now, and at last I had a better sense of their intentions. I submitted my letter of resignation to the board effective in two weeks.

The racial issues, my so-called liberal leanings, my close involvement with the Lynn family, and certainly my immaturity were factors in my departure from the work at the University of Memphis, but more than that, the eldership and I did not share a common vision of what was most important.

What next? I didn't know. I had always been able to work, so I knew I could get a job somewhere. I just didn't know where. Jim Woodroof's words were still fresh in my mind, as was another conversation I had a few months earlier with leaders at Harding. The church at Harding had contacted me about working with college students, and although it seemed clear to me that this was not a place I needed to be, out of respect for their invitation and the fact that I did not have a job, I contacted them to see if they were still interested. My call came at an interesting time for them; they were having a men's retreat in preparation for hiring someone new to work with their college students. I interviewed for the job and, after further thought and prayer, decided to accept the campus position.

We sold our house in Memphis immediately and found a new home in Searcy, Arkansas, beginning work on February 1, 1974, living and working closely with Jim. Our Sara had just turned five, and our second daughter, Missy, was three and a half. The next five and a half years were exciting ones for our family. First of all, I was given a mentor whom I did not know I needed. Jim and Louine Woodroof had five children, and Jim knew how to love and care for his family. He was the model I was looking for as a father and a husband. Of course, he was not perfect, but he was loving, compassionate, and present, and I learned much just by watching him. What's more, my faith grew in Jim's company. His fascination with the Sermon on the Mount, the best known of Jesus' addresses, continually inspired me, and I still draw strength from it today. Jim recently published a book, *Famous Sayings of Jesus*, which highlights the best relational teaching of Jesus' message of the Sermon on the Mount that I have ever read.

Even though Harding was a Christian institution set in a dry county where alcohol sales were prohibited, I knew that plenty was going on behind the scenes that people wanted hidden. I knew the rebels, and I knew how they thought. They were drinking beer, partying, and honky-tonkin' late at night fifty miles away in Little Rock. So many of these students who came from Christian homes didn't have a clue who Jesus was, and they didn't give a flip. At different times I asked them about their impression of Jesus the man. I just drew blank stares. They knew about religion, church, and the rules of what you can and cannot do, but they knew little about the real person of Christ. My assumptions that I'd expressed to Jim back in the fall were wrong. This place did have the kind of students I could serve.

"They knew about religion, church, and the rules of what you can and cannot do, but they knew little about the real person of Christ."

In many ways the work was far harder than that in Memphis. Many Harding students had seen so much toxic religion that they had become immune to anything spiritual. So many of them hated what they knew of God, and it was as if they had gone to a dinner all their lives but didn't realize that they had been eating the menu rather than the food itself. But I had tasted the steak, and I knew how good it was. I wanted all of them to eat well, and over the years many of them did.

Groups were formed to meet in homes near the campus during the week. There, students could build friendships and ask their hard spiritual questions without getting handed pat religious answers. These were safe places where they could talk about their real problems, and I found many students who shared my vision of the grace of God. They started to make an impact on their friends, reaching out to the students who were hurting or looking for something that made sense. By the end of our five years at Harding, students on every floor of every dorm were praying and looking out for students who might need a friend. They were there to encourage and support others.

We became a team. Jim was preaching weekly to more than 1,500 college students, and I helped run the small groups that put his messages into real-life action. Energy and joy were moving among the student body during that time, and we shared that energy and joy at home. Margaret Carol, whom we call Margy, was our third child, born April 4, 1975. She was a cotton top and had a wonderful, sweet presence. Charlotte loved being a homemaker and mother. These were precious times indeed.

CHAPTER NINE

I Am Broken

1979–1984

GROWING UP is hard enough when you are young, but when you are an adult with a family, a career, and people looking to you for advice and direction, the process of dealing with past wounds is more difficult. As a child, I had learned how to dance and sing, to smile and make people happy. By the time I was approaching my middle years, I had a far harder lesson in front of me. I still was not aware of the depths of my unconscious Messiah Complex that lurked below the surface. It would become full blown between 1979 and 1981. I wanted people to know the amazing love story between God and man that I had learned over these last nineteen years, but a hidden, unhealthy drive would threaten my personal life.

When I left the work in Memphis, I was younger and not trusted by the leaders, and there is no question that I would have been fired had I not resigned. Leaving Searcy was a different matter. My time in Searcy had been successful, but there was unrest in me. I felt a longing to reach out to folks beyond the Harding campus who didn't know the love of God. The leadership in Searcy loved Charlotte and me and the work we were doing with the students. Jim Woodroof had become a great mentor and friend. But I was captured by the vision shared by Landon Saunders—one where I would go to a metropolitan city far away and meet people who were broken by life and without hope.

Landon Saunders, president of Heartbeat, shared a vision with me of looking for teams of people who would be willing to reach out to love the broken and lonely. I was not sure who I would work for in this vision to go to the Northeast. I just knew I would begin a search for a metropolitan area to begin such a team.

"There is nothing on this planet more important than a human being." Landon spoke this truth often, and I believed it. Further, I was realizing that toxicity was too often present in religious settings. Love for people was the center of Christianity, and I wanted to be a part of pioneering a way to touch people with God's kindness. That impulse was altruistic and good. But the other impulse within me would cause serious trouble in the days to come. It was harmful to others, and ultimately it would have destroyed our family.

"There is nothing on this planet more important than a human being."

It was not supposed to be that way. I was an adult, approaching my forties with a beautiful wife and three beautiful daughters. We had been married more than fifteen years, and it never occurred to me that I was not completely grown up. But the evidence after we moved was undeniable. Something was not right. Life was not working as it was meant to. For eleven years, I struggled internally with hidden baggage that weighed me down. For eleven years, I struggled to grow up. The hidden reason I wanted to go to the lost and hurting was to gain significance and comfort for myself. That was part of the reason I wanted to leave Searcy and unearth a new adventure. Unfortunately, my hidden baggage traveled with us.

We arrived in New England in August 1979 with our yellow Volkswagen hitched to our creaking station wagon. These two vehicles contained all of us—three daughters, a cat, a dog, Charlotte's plants, and some of our worldly possessions—while a moving van followed with the rest. As we pulled into the driveway of our new home, a beautiful Dutch colonial house built in 1900, the future rose before us. The home was on three quarters of an acre with a beautiful lilac grove in the backyard. Sara was ten, Missy was nine, and Margy was four. Charlotte was thirty-six, and I had just turned thirty-seven. We had arrived in what for us felt like a new country, with a new home, a new work, and a fresh vision to serve people who were hurting. As far as beginnings went, this one felt good.

Jim Woodroof advised me to spend my first six months concentrating on getting the family settled into schools and the new home. I was determined to follow his advice, and I wanted to use the time to learn as much about the community as possible.

People were quick to educate us southerners about what life

was like in the North, explaining that there were two seasons in New England: winter and the Fourth of July. The cold was longer and deeper than any we had ever experienced in the South, and we were not prepared for it. The language was different, and the culture was foreign. Even though we were excited about the prospects ahead, we were surprisingly homesick for our close friends and loved ones in the South.

On walks in the cool of the evening, Charlotte would say, "Now tell me again why we moved to New England?" I would reply by sharing the vision that had propelled us there, our hope to make a difference in the lives of broken people and our desire to train others with the knowledge of how to build safe communities where people could grow physically, mentally, socially, emotionally, and spiritually.

The reality was that we were living in another culture, and it was hard. We came to Boston knowing no one, and they did not know us. The people there did not want to hear what we had to say until they saw in our lives something that made a connection with them. We were starting over relationally, and we missed the deep friendships of those who were dear to us far away. The conversations as we walked were difficult for both of us. Charlotte was grieving the loss of friends a thousand miles away while simultaneously wanting to be supportive of me. Internally, I was grieving the loss of the support network, but at the same time, I wanted to be strong for the work. I suffered in silence, just as I was trained to do as a child.

One reason we moved to the Boston area was to train leaders. We wanted to train as many of them as possible to help others work through difficult life issues. We had been inspired by the work that Landon was doing in this area. He partnered with us to put on a seminar near Boston titled "Feeling Good About Yourself." It was a three-night presentation in a public school, and we offered it free to the community. We purchased space on billboards and advertised on the radio and in the newspaper. Five or six hundred people joined us each night. We gave away books and tapes and invited people to join neighborhood groups to discuss the material. More than a hundred people signed up and met for twelve weeks. An anonymous donor gave $30,000 to run the event, and it was a resounding success. I was encouraged that we were making a difference in some lives, and Ruth was one of them.

Ruth was a forty-year-old Lithuanian refugee from the camps in WWII. She was depressed and desperate for help. One of our billboards advertising the seminar caught her attention. She attended, was impacted, and joined us in a follow-up twelve-week program afterward. Getting traction, she continued in a small study group focused on the book of John, finally joining one of our Life Groups. (They were small discussion groups formed to process issues of faith. Through safety, friendship, and good information, people were encouraged to think through life-and-death options.) She discovered the joy of reading the Bible for the first time. Within a year, Ruth had dedicated her life to God and become much more stable emotionally.

Six months later, terminal cancer struck, and Ruth was told she had less than a year to live. She accepted that peacefully, and we all prayed for her healing. By the grace of God, she was completely healed, and today she writes some of the best poetry I have ever read. She is a dear person.

Ruth had three children, the youngest a little older than our Margy. Years later, her eighteen-year-old daughter was killed in a car of speeding teenagers. The memorial service was in the parish of St. Malachy's in Burlington, Massachusetts. The service affirmed Ruth's love of God and her true hope of reunion with her daughter because of the life after death promised by Christ. It was a powerful moment of hope for the people who were in such grief.

To be involved in the life of a person like Ruth was a privilege, but with the work came a lot more responsibility, and my underlying Messiah Complex began to kick in with even greater force. Within two years of arriving in the North, I had two hundred names on my daily prayer list. I refused to pray for them in bulk. No, I promised to pray for them by name, so that's what I did. I didn't want to let anyone down. The growing internal pressure was not caused just by the time that it took to pray for each one; it was the feeling that I was responsible for all of them, as if it was up to me and me alone to battle for them and secure their healing. I was

"I was overextending myself again, and my family and I were paying the price."

overextending myself again, and my family and I were paying the price.

I hit the wall, and I hit it hard. The energy and joy that had filled my life over the previous twenty years vanished without a trace. I felt weary, burdened, and overwhelmed in ways that I had never felt before. The interns living with us became a source of added stress, and my mornings spent alone with God no longer left me feeling refreshed and inspired for the day ahead. Instead, I emerged from these times feeling overburdened. What little joy and life I was holding onto were being sucked out from the pores of my skin.

"I no longer felt the closeness of God, and my world stopped making sense."

I no longer felt the closeness of God, and my world stopped making sense. I journaled a lot, looking for some kind of perspective that would illuminate what was happening to me.

January 27, 1981

Lord, I need help. Something is not going right! I need your help. Do I really want to be faithful to you? What are you trying to teach me right now? Where am I missing it? My heart is drawn to people. I see the pain. I feel the emptiness in their lives. My heart grieves—then I realize that I am causing my own family suffering. They don't seem to understand that I long to be with them, too. My heart and soul need your support, O God—My weakness is always before me. . . . It makes me feel like I want to run away from it all. You call us to suffer—What is that suffering?

February 8, 1981

Dear Father,
There is so much I do not understand! There is so much I want to understand. I think about the people, Lord—All the lonely people—longing for something—Help me get to them. I know, O Lord, the battle has just begun here!!

For my family, I cried, *O, Father, you have given me three precious children—I want you to raise them to honor, adore and praise your matchless name!! Help me to walk with them in understanding. Lord, help me to lift up Charlotte—grant her peace, O God.*

In the summer of 1981, Mama called. She had phoned Daddy and talked to him for the first time in thirty-one years. She told me how the conversation started.

"Hello, Sidney, this is Mildred. Please don't hang up."

No response on the other end.

"Are you still there, Sidney?"

"Yes. And I'm not going to hang up."

They talked some, but there was no way I would see my childhood dream of united parents come true.

The heaviness of my family of origin pressed down on me. I felt the need to be deeply involved with my family. I had the education and training, and I felt the responsibility to help others, but especially my own family. Daddy and my stepmother, Mary, were headed for divorce, and I was trying to help them reconcile. I had hundreds of people on my prayer list, and I was so overwhelmed and weary that I could hardly speak. There was something wrong inside me, and I needed relief.

Intellectual questions weighed me down. I was searching for answers, reading great writers and reflecting on my beliefs and presuppositions. I was determined that I would not throw out what I believed unless I found something better with which to replace it, but my foundations had been shaken. This was the real beginning of a total new awareness of self. For the first ten years of my work, I had been with college students and had a large support group. Now, I was working with older adults as well as college students and people with trauma—a broad spectrum of developmental and personality issues. I was directing the Resource Center for Life that provided counseling and seminars in the community on building quality relationships. Although I knew the story of Jesus, I was becoming aware that I did not know myself.

"Although I knew the story of Jesus, I was becoming aware that I did not know myself."

But there were so many other stories around, and they were filled with such pain. There was the father whose teenage son had died, a young man who was paralyzed from the neck down, a twenty-one-year-old college student who attempted suicide, and many others. I was there for all of them—always wanting to help in these helpless situations but feeling that I was never able to give enough. Daddy and my stepmother were going through a divorce after twenty-seven years. I was with Daddy as he told my stepmother that the marriage was over and that he had found someone else. I felt guilty that I could not save their marriage.

Her response shocked me: "If you leave me, I will kill myself, and you will have to live with that the rest of your life."

I remember looking Mary in the eye and saying to her, "Mom, if you kill yourself, let me tell you what I am going to do. I am going to make sure Daddy knows he is not responsible."

I felt like I was in a snake pit.

For the next three years, the presence of God seemed gone, and I did not know why. This dark night of my soul lasted from 1981 to 1984, even though early in the period I felt as though I had discovered a way out.

During the summer of 1981, Charlotte, the girls, and I took a six-week trip to New Mexico to visit Charlotte's family. The day before my thirty-ninth birthday I was walking in the open semi-desert of New Mexico. My head was full of one thought: *What do I really want?* My inner world was shaken, and my view of myself was not clear. I thought I had things figured out before I went to New England. I thought I was equipped to meet the real traumas of the world, but I was unable to deal with the massive cumulative brokenness I was experiencing.

Life was not abundant. Something was happening inside me that I could not explain or escape. It was a dark place. I kept thinking, *Do I want to stay this way or change? And if I want to change, do I want to do so by putting this lifelessness behind me and forget about it, or do I want to get to the root of the problem?* I was afraid to face these questions, afraid of where the honest answers might lead me. But I decided to try. So I asked myself again: *What do you really want for your life?* In light of my family history the possibility of trying to bury the pain was real. I would be very capable of getting relief through my addictive personality, just as both parents had.

Four answers came in a moment of clarity on that ninth day of July, 1981:

1. I want to think clearly.
2. I want to walk securely.
3. I want to live boldly.
4. I want to love faithfully.

These twenty words set me on a new path of discovery—a journey that would take me inside to the world of my soul, down into the darkness shrouded by death. In time, the working out of these four simple statements would change everything about my life, eventually leaving me relieved, settled, and renewed. In time, these words would help me focus on four practical solutions to my current problems. I wanted to use my mind and think as clearly as possible. I wanted to live with that internal security of joy I had tasted over the previous twenty years. I wanted to live life to the fullest and model for my children how to get all there is out of life. Finally, I wanted to love my wife faithfully, to love my children and those who were near and dear in my life. I loved Charlotte deeply, and the pressure inside me was coming from a fragmentation of my soul to which I would have to attend each morning. I knew there was an unconscious self. I just did not know my own story yet. I was too busy trying to save others.

I continued to be convinced that the Wisdom Literature in the Bible—Psalms, Proverbs, Ecclesiastes, Job, and the Song of Songs—offered the kind of thinking that I could trust. I turned to them daily and read other challenging and thought-provoking books. Meanwhile, our family had grown with the arrival of our fourth child, Ashley Elizabeth, born October 25, 1983.

"I was experiencing burnout, and I was toxic."

But I was experiencing burnout, and I was toxic. Each evening as we gathered together for supper, I told them some of the places and stories from my day, detailing the broken lives that I had witnessed. My intention was that they would learn from the horrible darkness I was seeing. I was hoping they would be able to avoid some of these mistakes, but I was blind to the fact that my words were not helping. My timing was bad related to their ages. I was not being present with them, not giving them what they needed—a father instead of a spiritual traffic cop. Yet I could not stop. Something in me was driving me. It was my unconscious fear and overresponsibility, and I was pushing them away rather than inviting them into the joy I intended.

As a safeguard to build family memories, we instituted a practice of taking the family to the beach or to the mountains before each school year. It was in 1982 that I gave my children permission to tell me how they thought I was doing as a dad. They told me the truth, and it hurt. The one thing on which I prided myself the most was the thing for which they criticized me: "Dad," they said, "you're just too religious."

It was so hard to hear that from them, especially because I was sure that one of the primary causes of damage to the people with whom I had spent so many years working was religion. My daughters' words cut my legs out from under me, and I asked them what I could do to improve. They said, "Dad, you need to lighten up."

The next year we repeated the trip, and I repeated the question: "How am I doing as a dad?" They said that I was doing better. Each week, I had a date with each daughter, doing something special with each one. I stopped telling stories of people's broken lives at the dinner table and tried to keep things lighter in their world. Charlotte was wonderful during this time as we sat down for meals together as a family. We were faithful every year to go to the mountains or to the beach before the beginning of the school year for fun and games and family sharing. The girls reminded me that there was still room for improvement, but I appeared to be getting better.

Around this time, a new book was published that changed the way many people viewed the world. M. Scott Peck's *The Road Less Traveled* made a big impact on me. It identified two personality types, suggesting that we all lean toward one or the other: (1) the neurotic persona who has the tendency to blame oneself when things go wrong, and (2) the person who suffers from a character disorder that lays blame on others. I knew at once that I lean toward the first sort, the neurotic, and Charlotte and I still joke that, when something goes wrong, I think it is my fault. And Charlotte agrees. M. Scott Peck stated that *there would be no emotional or spiritual growth until a person took full responsibility for his or her life.* This statement resonated deeply with me. A spotlight illuminated my overwhelming sense of responsibility for other people. I realized this was a definite problem area in my life.

While living and working in the area, I decided to enroll in a doctorate program at Boston University. I knew I needed to explore new avenues for my personal development as well as gain additional knowledge that would help others. The Psychodynamics of Marriage and the Family courses gave me the opportunity to look back on three distinct periods: early childhood, preadolescence, and teen years. How had they shaped me? My first seven years of life were largely defined by the secure, nurturing neighborhood of south Memphis where I felt like the favored child of the Roseberry family. Then came the period of confusion, chaos, and divorce that lasted from the age of seven to twelve. The third period, from twelve to eighteen years old, was influenced by Daddy's decision to allow an emotionally unsafe, jealous, hostile, and tense atmosphere to enter our home by way of my deeply insecure stepmother. I mapped it all out with graphs and letters and submitted it as part of my doctoral study. But the real value of this learning was the light it cast into my internal world. One of the tools in psychotherapy is the genogram, which is used in counseling to map pathological illness through the generations of a family. I wrote my own story using a genogram. Later, I drew on the genogram as I developed a tool to help people with their family issues. (See more about this later in this book.)

"I was learning so much about myself in the process, becoming ever more aware of the lies that I had grown to believe."

I took courses in branches of psychiatry and biblical studies, learning how healing happens within the individual and exploring the context in which the story of Jesus played out. These two streams of study flowed closely together, one informing the other.

For five years, I studied the complexities of human personality while simultaneously engaged in intensive counseling and group psychodynamics. I was learning so much about myself in the process, becoming ever more aware of the lies that I had grown to believe and built my life upon. They may have been good and well-meaning for me as a child, but now they were deeply toxic to my soul.

Believing that I had to "be good" in order to be secure and survive, "perform to please" in order to gain esteem, "be strong" and "show no weakness" in order to have control—these had become the drivers in my life, particularly when I was under pressure. Of the three, the false belief that I must "be good" was the one that got me into the most trouble. It could easily have been translated as "I am responsible to make others okay," and it lay at the heart of my overresponsibility and my Messiah Complex. It also fed my pride, although I had trouble seeing it because I was working so hard to make things better for others. How could that selflessness really be pride? The motivation behind it went all the way back to the little boy who needed to take care of his daddy; the more I helped people, the better person I was.

I had learned to value myself through my achievements, through lives helped, through courses run, and through prayer lists prayed from start to finish. The years of training in Boston made me painfully aware that I was failing to pull any of this off. They left me crushed but ready to be rebuilt. Despite the revelations and the sense that God was unearthing some vital issues for me, I was still a mess.

In some ways, realizing that I was a mess was both a shock and a release. Whatever I was feeling, I needed to process early each morning in order to make it through the day. My daughter Sara asked me: "Daddy, why do you get up so early every morning?"

"Because," I replied, "I am broken inside. I have to put on my braces every morning."

"Daddy, why do you get up so early every morning?"

"Because," I replied, "I am broken inside. I have to put on my braces every morning."

My beliefs told me that I should expect a lot from myself. I took seriously the words of the Apostle John when he wrote, "Those who say they live in God should live their lives as Jesus did." Every day I made the effort to do just that, and yet I never felt that I fully achieved it. I kept thinking, *I must save the person! It is up to me*. Perhaps that was the breakthrough I needed—to know that it was okay for me not to be perfect. Was this the beginning of the end of my Messiah Complex, the gradual realization that I was never going to be able to act like the Messiah himself?

If only it were that simple.

At first, I did not know why I was not doing well emotionally. I was failing in ways I never dreamed I would fail. Up to that point, my adult life had been so full of good relationships and a feeling of warmth and love. Now I just felt heavy inside, feeling that something was wrong with me but unable to name the wrong. In the early morning, I felt this brokenness, and I had to be very deliberate not to bring a heaviness to Charlotte and the children. Thankfully, I was not experiencing deep mood swings. Charlotte experienced me as consistent with a steady, stable mood. My pattern through the years had been to deal with things on my own and not burden others with my innermost feelings. Most of the time, I did not have language for these feelings anyway. Looking through my early morning journals, I realized my journal was like a friend to whom I tried to express my emotional confusion. I felt safe—just me and God. My strength was that I knew the love of God. My weakness was that I did not know my own story and the depth of my internal, unconscious deceptions.

So much of the person I had become and the choices I made were founded on a series of lies. I believed that I was responsible, that I was duty bound to stay the course beyond all others. The trouble with building a life on lies is that these false beliefs bury themselves within, so far down in the darkness of the subconscious that just identifying them can seem like a lifelong task. And so, in the middle of the most difficult period of my adult life, I searched for a way out. I had learned that naming these lies would be vital, and I knew that becoming aware of these lies, naming them, exposing them for all to see, confessing them openly, turning from them, and replacing them with the God-blessed truth would be the greatest thing I could do.

History tells us that life is hard and treacherous at times, leaving us surprised by tragedy and often struggling to find a way of being at peace with the world around us. We find it hard not to repeat history and hard to let go of resentment, depression, failure, despair, hatred, judgment, and death. For me and for so many others, the healing process started by looking back to what is called the family of origin. Mine is riddled with the darkness of a family system of adultery, alcoholism, divorce, attempted suicide, abandonment, and children left to fend for themselves emotionally and spiritually. At age eighteen, I realized I was capable of any evil under certain circumstances.

As I looked back, I recalled how, from the time I was seven years old, I experienced a hidden desperation that began to lift at the age of eighteen. Only after getting drunk that night at Ole Miss was I able to wake up the next day and see that, unless I made a change, I was going to die. It was not that I had become an alcoholic. After all, it was only one night. But I knew from the patterns I had observed in my family that this path led to one final destination. Mama was an alcoholic, my grandfather was an alcoholic; it ruined them, and it would ruin me too.

"The healing process started by looking back to what is called the family of origin."

Change can come quickly sometimes. It came quickly for me on that hung-over morning at Ole Miss. But it was only possible because I could see the problem, the cause, and the potential risk. With the troubles that plagued my adult soul, the process was far harder.

I was born into a world of secrets and lies that did little more than rob the people I loved from living a life of freedom and love. This is the map I was given, one marked with too many dangers to name, with pain too deep to describe, and the only mechanism of coping being to numb whatever feelings threatened to reach the surface. They chose alcohol; I chose to perform my way out of the mess. Perhaps mine was less destructive and more socially acceptable, but it was destructive all the same.

Each of us has a story. Every one of us adopts certain beliefs that we use to help us make our way through life's treacherous journey. And for a while they appear to work. Most often we take on the beliefs when we are children, and at some point we must acknowledge that we have outgrown our childhood ways. At some point on the journey, these childhood beliefs—so often around issues of security and survival, affection and esteem, and power and control—will

"Every one of us adopts certain beliefs to help us make our way through life's treacherous journey. And for a while, they appear to work."

start to rob a person of joy. This is when change must happen before it's too late.

Despite so desperately wanting not to repeat my family history, I still marched to the beat of my childhood drum. I found within me a longing to build relationships where love was at the center, to have a home where there would be peace, to create a safe and joyful place for my children to experience a mom and a dad who really loved each other. These are great aims to have, but I added to mine the toxic tendency toward overresponsibility. I wanted to build this type of family, and I was going to be the perfect dad. Or else.

The lie that bound me was this: if I wanted my children to make it in life, I had to teach them to be good—just like me. Their only way forward on this perilous journey, one in which families like mine were easy prey for betrayal, alcoholism, and suicide, was to place their feet in the tracks I left behind. Their comments about my appearing too religious were shocking. At first I tried to alter my outward behavior, changing my language a little and modifying my actions from time to time. Unfortunately, I was not dealing with the heart of the matter.

Meanwhile, my family was clearly wounded. Their woundedness came from my focus on helping others outside the home, particularly since I was not fully equipped to help some in the way they needed. I thought the way to help everyone was to model how to "be good," but the message sent to them was that I was trying to meet people in their humanity with my piety. I was working hard, thinking it was my responsibility to help fix the problems I was seeing in people, *but my core belief was wrong.* Looking back, I would not call it working hard but working dumb. The emotional energy I had to put into taking care of others left me inattentive to Charlotte's and the children's needs. Charlotte suffered, my children suffered, and I was in an internal unconscious battle. I modeled for my children how to count others but not count yourself. One of my daughters describes herself the same way. She says, "I know how to take care of others better than I do myself."

I was fixated on being there for others, oblivious to the negative consequences of what appeared on the surface to be a good thing. An example was my attempt to help a minister friend in trouble. I failed to be there for him in the way he needed me. He has written an insightful book that speaks of the three years we worked together. Clearly, I was ill-equipped to do my part; I didn't know how to be with him in an effective way as he moved through one of the most difficult periods in his personal journey: an extramarital affair, the loss of his ministry, and separation from his children by a distance of two thousand miles. Thankfully, others were able to provide a loving, compassionate presence that made a difference for him in those years. He is now one of my closest friends and a mentor on my personal journey.

Sadly, as our time at Boston drew to a close when I was forty-seven years old, I still had not quite learned the lesson that would be a key to my healing—or rather, I had not yet fully absorbed it. It was clear to me that my effectiveness in helping people was limited. I did not understand exactly why, but I knew I needed a change. I thought it might be time to go back South to more familiar roots. Perhaps things would be better down home. And for a while, they were.

The Soul Wound

No one knows the pain
Of the soul wound of others
But I can listen

I will not give up
Seeking to participate
In loving others

Only two commands matter
Loving God is the first one
Loving each other is next
Give me a pure heart

The deepest soul wound
Unspeakable tragedy
Is understood by your God
He shares the same wound

Betrayed by his friends
Who thought they knew who they were
Jealousy and strife
They were awakened by love
Friendship indescribable

This story I tell
After listening to the wound
The soul wound fully expressed
Given space to heal
In the safety of true friends
Peace passes understanding

Terry S. Smith
June 27, 2013

PART FOUR

The past is never dead. It's not even past.

—*William Faulkner*

CHAPTER TEN

I Am a Father, Not a Messiah

1984–1989

A LITTLE BOY learns to ride a bicycle only one way—by falling off and getting up. He falls off and must get up again and again and again. The pattern repeats. From afar, the little boy seems stuck in the loop. Until one moment, an almost magical one, he becomes free and rides the bike without hitting the dirt.

The illustration made me smile. I was reading a book by the noted Chinese evangelist, Watchman Nee, while on vacation with the family in a cabin on a lake in New Hampshire in August 1984. It was a beautiful week, full of games of tennis and other activities. But inside, I still felt heavy and pressured.

On holiday in New Hampshire, I decided to read just two books: the New Testament and *Against the Tide* by Watchman Nee. Nee's biography fascinated me, especially his simple illustration of the boy and the bicycle. He used it to describe the growth of young Christians, and I laughed as I read it. I knew it to be true, and it resonated with me, but why? I was not a new Christian, and I was certainly no stranger to riding free in my faith. It was a mystery to me.

"God was saying that he wanted to bust the hitch on my wagon and let him do the carrying."

One morning after the vacation, I was preparing for a class where I would teach on chapter 19 of the book of John, and the significance of Nee's illustration hit me. Yes, I had known what it is like to ride free, but I had hooked a wagon onto my bike and put people in it. When they fell out, I felt guilty—convinced that it was all my fault. I felt as if God was saying that he wanted to bust the hitch on my wagon and let him do the carrying. I was stunned, and I knew what

I was seeing was true. With the sudden insight and in a split second, I was able to bust the hitch on my wagon. I shared what had happened with my class that very morning. We had been in Boston for five years, and had I not discovered this major insight, I probably would have resigned under the pressure. We lived five more years in Boston.

"I was beginning to realize God had not put these heavy burdens on me; I had put them on myself. I was beginning to get a glimpse of freedom."

I was beginning to realize God had not put these heavy burdens on me; I had put them on myself. I was beginning to get a glimpse of freedom. There were so many ways I had shortchanged my daughters during their growing-up years. Although I had been well intentioned, I had been misguided and distracted. There were moments of grace but great stretches of blindness.

One morning, I dropped Sara off at school and told her I would pick her up at the large rock that rested in front of the middle school at 3:00 p.m. She was twelve years old, and her leg was in a cast as a result of a car crash. At 3:30 p.m., I looked at the clock in my counseling room and realized with horror that I had forgotten all about her. I jumped up, apologized to the person I was trying to help, and rushed over to the school. I got there, but Sara was nowhere to be found.

I got home, and there she was, lying on the couch, steaming mad. I knelt beside her and asked her to forgive me. Her face was tight, and she would not look at me or speak a word to me.

Right before she went to sleep that evening, I went to her room and again knelt beside her and asked her: "What was it like for you when I did not keep my word to pick you up at school today?"

"I thought I was special to you," she stammered, turning to me with hurt and anger in her face. "You promised me you would be there. Where were you, and how could you do this to me?"

She was a great reader, and she was very competent in her verbal and emotional skills. She had all the language she needed and used it as she went on to describe the pain she felt at my failure to show up for her. I wept. I felt her pain and grieved my failure to the one I professed to love. There was no excuse. In tears and still on my knees, I asked her again to forgive me. She wrapped her little twelve-year-old arms around my neck and held me tight, saying,

"Daddy, I forgive you."

Missy was our laid-back tiger. She was quiet, submissive, and always wanted to please us. I remember asking her how she always made As in her classes. She said she pretended that she was the teacher. We saw her aggressive, fighting spirit when she was on the athletic field. She played field hockey, which is a very physical contact sport. After her first game, she came home in tears.

"Missy, why are you crying?"

She said, "I made my first goal. But it was for the other team!"

I encouraged her not to take herself so seriously. She took my advice. I came into the room later, and she was leaning over a bowl of chocolate chip ice cream.

I said, "Missy, what are you doing?"

"I'm celebrating my first goal!"

Sara was just a year ahead of Missy. They were friends, and Sara had so many friends that Missy never had to make any effort to develop friends, partially because Sara always paved the way. Missy was easygoing, beautiful, and very lovable.

Margy was our quiet one. She was the thinker and five years younger than Missy. For eight years, she was the baby of the family. When she found out our fourth child was on the way, she ran to her room and cried. Her place as the baby was being taken. I think I missed being with Margy the most because she never demanded any attention. She liked to stay in her room and read, and I failed to draw her out. My interpretation was that I didn't want to invade her space, but also my overextended personality kept me busy helping others and not really seeing Margy and her need for special time.

One special moment with Margy happened soon after we moved to Burlington. It was a brisk Saturday afternoon in the fall. The leaves on the trees were bursting in shades of yellow and orange. Usually, it would have been football game time for me. But Charlotte and I had decided we were not going to have a TV in the house until we decided together what place it would have in the family. I was feeling the frustration of this restriction and sulked to my bedroom to be quiet and get in touch with my feelings. In the quiet, I began to read in Psalms and meditate. After an hour of solitude, I heard a light knock on the door. It was Margy.

"Daddy, will you play with me?"

My first thought was, *I am having an amazing time alone here with God. How can I interrupt this moment?* But as quickly as the first thought came, another stronger thought riveted my soul: *I want you to go do with your daughter what I have just done with you. Go be with her!* I rose immediately, and we went outside. I played all afternoon with Margy and her two older sisters. That was a teachable moment for me because if I had been watching the football game, I would have played with them only during halftime.

Elizabeth was the baby born in 1983 in Winchester, Massachusetts. She was a joy. With her birth we had two teenagers, one preadolescent, and a baby. Elizabeth was always active and sharp. When she was about five years old, I was talking with her, looking her in the eye, but my mind was elsewhere.

"Daddy, you are not listening to me!" She could see I was distracted.

The day after Christmas, 1985, I had a special date to the movies with sixteen-year-old Sara. As we stood in the line waiting to buy the tickets, I overheard the girls in front of me say that they did not have enough money to get in the theater. They just needed fifty cents. I immediately gave a quarter and the man next to me who heard the same thing gave them a quarter.

Then he said this to me, "I was supposed to be here with my wife, but she is out with another man."

I turned, looked him in the eye, and said to him, "I heard what you said. That is really hard." Then I proceeded to purchase our tickets and headed into the theater. I turned to him and asked if he wanted to sit with us. Sara, who was in front of me, rolled her eyes, hardly believing I had invited this man to sit with us. After the movie I invited him home for tea. Sara waited till we got to the car and said with fearful passion: "Daddy, he could kill us!"

Jack, a captain in the U.S. Air Force, came home with us, and in a way, Sara was right. Later, he attempted suicide, went through a divorce, and yet after two years, went on to hope and healing. I discovered these occurrences were paradoxical. On the one hand, people were helped. But on the other, I was sending a silent message to my children: others were more important than they were.

"I rationalized that they would be all right because, according to my thinking, they had it so much better than what I experienced."

In spite of my shortcomings, I enjoyed these years with the family. Charlotte was the anchor in the house, and our relationship seemed to flourish. We were busy with the children in the schools, the church community, and the Burlington community. I was busy manning the Resource Center, seeing people, and working with those in crisis.

So how much damage had I done to my children? One thought of consolation and comfort was that I did not leave them like Mama left us. I was able to be present with them in ways Daddy never was with me. I rationalized that they would be all right because, according to my thinking, they had it so much better than what I experienced. Surely my failures would be insignificant by comparison.

Some of that thinking was right, but most of it was wrong. Yes, they have been able to figure out their lives without me. But the second part was wrong. I did cause them damage, and I needed to face that fact for my sake and theirs.

These days, my children and I are close, and my love for them flows with far fewer barriers and obstacles than it did when they were young. I know that I failed each of them in different ways, and I know that God has forgiven me. I know that my children have forgiven me. And I also know this: forgiveness is the most difficult place to reach in a human life. It is the most treacherous journey on the planet.

"Forgiveness is the most difficult place to reach in a human life."

After the bicycle and wagon revelation, I began to cut off certain people for whom I had taken on too much responsibility. This was a literal word from God for me. After this, I was freer internally, and I knew renewal was happening inside me. The internal freedom allowed me to continue pursuing my doctoral studies and eventually receive my doctorate in Personality, Religion, and Culture.

CHAPTER ELEVEN

I Am Failing Worse than I Have Ever Failed Before

1989–1994

If my greatest strength was my greatest weakness, then my pride was my greatest enemy. In 1989 we arrived in Searcy, where I would direct the Family Life and Counseling Center near the Harding campus. The school's church hired me for the position. I was making a lot of headway in gaining personal insight, but I could not see my arrogance. It was there all the same. In my mind we had just completed ten successful years in metropolitan Boston, and I was back on my home turf, having learned a lot through those years. I had learned to draw healthy boundaries and was able to help numerous people on their personal journeys.

I had been accepted into the doctoral program at Boston University under the supervision of Dr. Merle Jordan, the best possible person in the country for this task. I had devoured his book *Taking on the Gods: The Task of the Pastoral Counselor*, and I was eager to learn more. But in truth, I was excited to display my gifts. I didn't think I had much more to learn. I was blinded, and I had absolutely no idea of the extent of my pride. Dr. Jordan was my supervisor, and he pointed out my blind spots that were emerging from written verbatims I gave to him as part of his supervision of my counseling work. Intellectually I knew about those blind spots, but emotionally I was having a harder time accepting them at a gut level.

Although I had made progress, I still hadn't fully dealt with the root of my overdeveloped sense of responsibility. That mutated childhood gift of being able to take care of myself and those around me was about to be clearly exposed for the failure it was. I was about to take another step in the learning process. I was about to confront my core toxic belief.

Perhaps if I had listened to the symbolic dream I had one night just before we arrived back in Searcy, some of what followed might have been different. This dream came after spending a week at the Washington School of Psychiatry. In the dream, I was in a therapy group with many wounded personalities; it was a mess. The room was filled with human brokenness. There were people dealing with alcoholism and all kinds of personal abuse, and I felt completely overwhelmed. I was suffocating, and the waste kept piling higher and higher. It was my job to lead the group to bring about healing, but instead of feeling the joy and peace that should come from that, I felt only stress. I was so glad to wake up from that dream and put it behind me. Little did I know that was precisely where I was headed.

"In the dream, I was in a therapy group with many wounded personalities; it was a mess."

Initially, it felt good to be back in the Harding community. Searcy was a small university town—and still is. It is small enough to have a strong sense of community. I was committed to giving my best to the community, and we knew a lot of folks there. My pride might not have allowed me to admit it, but I felt I was coming back as a seasoned veteran, fully equipped to offer myself in God's service. Humbly, of course.

I began directing the counseling center. I had completed all my course work for the doctorate while in Boston, but I still needed to complete my dissertation. I wanted to explore the ways group work could help people; I knew that healing often came when people felt safe in a group of people who could accept and love them *in spite of their weaknesses*. So I started looking for people who felt likewise, and I heard suggestions that I meet a couple who had a lot of experience in the area, Dr. Bill Verkler and his wife, Billie. She was renowned as the best psychodramatist in that part of the country. I had met them in 1962 when I transferred from Ole Miss to Harding. They had been pioneers in working with African American churches when Harding was not integrated and Ole Miss was experiencing the turmoil of forced integration.

In Searcy, the Verklers were leading groups in the community center with the outcasts of the county. They were working with the last, the least, the lost, the poorest, and the least loved. I asked if I could join them in their work, and they invited me to participate. In an amazing way, they were able to create a safe environment and take people in the direction of healing. Mrs. Verkler was brilliant in relating to people who were broken, and she and her husband often took people into their home. Their house was about five miles out in the country on eighty acres of land.

Psychodrama is a powerful therapeutic technique in which a person brings up a past trauma and tells the group about the experience. People are chosen to play different roles, and the scene is reenacted in front of the one who was traumatized. The person relives the event in the presence of friends and experiences their support and care. The group then processes the trauma, talking about it and sharing it. Over the years, I have seen remarkable outcomes.

Consider this as a simple example of what would happen. The scenario is about a little girl who has a traumatic experience at the dinner table when her father disciplines her severely for spilling her milk. We would reenact that event with the child thinking that she is no good and the father being angry. In the group she would experience that all over again. But this time the father tells his daughter, "I was wrong. You're not bad for spilling the milk. It was an accident." We would reframe the event in a healthy way with the father handling it in the right way and not shaming her or causing her to feel guilt.

Billie was loving, eccentric, creative, and brilliant. She felt some people at Harding had taken advantage of her generosity. Intuitively discerning, she often saw fake Christianity and religiosity in a very religious town. Others might have been fooled but not Billie. Sometimes she exposed the hypocrisy that she saw around her, and that caused some hostility and suspicion to build within the church community.

Bill and Billie were enthusiastic when I asked them to join me at the counseling center. I wanted them to train me so I could do what they had been doing with groups. It seemed a personal opportunity as well as a chance to work on my dissertation for Boston University. We invited a group to join us in a three-hour session every Monday evening—twelve people with whom I already was working, as well as a few of the Verklers' patients. This spilled over into personal consultations during the week with the various group members, and Billie and I frequently worked together as a team. It was a deeply complicated and emotional group: two members had been in satanic cults, and one had been sexually abused by her father and a priest when she was a little girl. Dr. Verkler had his Ph.D. in Sociology and could chart the personal progress of individuals. What was supposed to run for fourteen weeks ended up carrying on for three years!

Whenever Billie entered a room, her presence was immediately noticeable because of the warmth and love she exuded. She could read a person like a book with incredible results. In psychodrama, one technique is to "double" a person, which involves standing behind a person and putting into words what the person is feeling in ways the person cannot. Billie was amazingly gifted; she was on target 99 percent of the time, and people naturally wanted to follow up and talk with her in greater depth. She knew exactly how to meet people where they were, and she moved them gently to the next step.

But these were hard times for me. Throughout the three years, I relived my story. My past surfaced with a vengeance. Such was the intensity of the group that I was introduced to the diagnosis of multiple personalities, that is, a person has been so traumatized as a child that he or she has an out-of-body experience. The person dissociates from the actual physical or emotional abuse so that she has no memory of the event taking place until she is much older. Later, the memory will begin to surface.

"Our goal was to provide a safe place with good information and a trained therapist."

Our goal was to provide a safe place with good information and a trained therapist who could provide a way for the person to heal. We knew it would take time, but we were committed. And at the end of our time, many members of the group were helped and healed. I was worse, however. Although I was aware of this problem in Boston, a deep-seated trauma related to my overresponsibility surfaced in a new way, the result of the perfect storm of relationships that made up the group.

There was another side to my work with the Verklers. It was a side of which I am not proud, but looking back, I realize it took this trauma to surface the depth of my false beliefs. The truth is that things went wrong with my work with them, in particular with my relationship with Billie. She was a woman of good character, highly educated with a master's degree in education. She was very skilled at teaching children and training teachers. And yet the religious community of which I was a part considered her an outcast. People viewed her as an exuberant eccentric, who often made them uncomfortable.

The counseling center I was directing was supported by the church community I had been a part of ten years earlier in Searcy. The board of directors was not pleased that I had brought in the Verklers to join me. The board's criticism of the Verklers seemed wrong to me, and I resolved, however unintentionally, to counter the rejection. I was emotionally bound, wanting desperately for the Verklers to be acknowledged and recognized for their good work. I was offended on their behalf and felt responsible for them, especially for Billie.

Billie began to confide in me as I shared with her about my experiences. My old Messiah Complex kicked in, and as a friend and not a counselor, I wanted to help heal her wounds. Dr. Verkler encouraged me because he saw that I treated her with respect and provided an opportunity for her gifting to be used. We had a mutual understanding of childhood traumas.

The Verklers had become critical players in the completion of my doctoral dissertation project, which had been approved by Boston University. My project was titled "The Use of Psychodrama in a Conservative Church." Each member of my board of directors received a copy when I completed the dissertation so they would know more about what we were doing. I hoped they might finally see the healing results of our work together and acknowledge the Verklers for their work. Much to my surprise, the dissertation only confirmed to the church leaders that I was too involved with the Verklers.

Looking back, I can see that I not only wanted the leaders of the congregation to acknowledge her gifts and use her, but I also began to feel that I ought to increasingly include Billie in my family. We were spending so much time together: the groups on Monday nights, the follow-up meetings with the various individual group members as they felt the need, and the work to get the project in line with my dissertation. It started to cause strain on my relationship with Charlotte and even the children. Billie phoned me at home, wanting to talk through a certain issue that was current in the group or that related to the project. I felt trapped between not wanting to add to her sense of rejection and not wanting to remove myself again from my family.

Meanwhile, Dr. Verkler continued to encourage my relationship with Billie, and the three of us worked well together. She sought counseling from me as we processed issues, and I had become dependent on the two of them in regard to my dissertation. The tension rose as I struggled to have the community see her as the gifted therapist she was. I wanted to use her in the counseling center. But as a result, I felt trapped.

Charlotte was candid with me about the amount of time I was spending with Billie on the phone in the evening, describing her as just "too much." I knew she was right, but I absolutely did not want to be yet another person to pull away from the Verklers, and so I remained in close contact.

"My unconscious, false perform-to-please-others self was strong."

My unconscious, false perform-to-please-others self was strong. Although I felt no sexual attraction toward Billie, the misplaced feelings of responsibility were strong enough to create a serious problem at home and within me. I treated her like a family member, better even than I was treating my own family at times. I gave her what I thought was the very best I could give—my unwavering attention and support. I was wrong to act this way, but she valued me, she esteemed me, and she made me feel that I mattered. My deep need to be needed, the old assumptions about the importance of my being good and not letting anyone down, plus the pride in being the only one to stick by her—*all collided to make a toxic internal mess.*

The way I saw it, her work with people was empowering and God-centered. *How could others not see the truth as I did? If I would only work a little harder with her and her husband, the church leaders were bound to accept them.* The tension got higher at home, and the tension got greater between Billie, Dr. Verkler, and me. I was not measuring up to Charlotte's expectations as a husband. I was not able to give what I thought Billie and her husband needed, and besides that, the board of leaders who had hired me communicated to me that I was not doing the job they hired me to do. I had sixty-four people on a waiting list, and I was working harder than I had ever worked before. Does this sound familiar?

Our two oldest daughters had left for college. Margy was in her critical teen years, and Elizabeth was still a young child. I missed both of them. Looking back and talking with Charlotte, I realize I was so preoccupied with my work that I was not present with them the way they needed me at important times in their lives.

"I was so locked into my old patterns that I was deaf and blind to the truth."

The tragic thing for me was that I was feeling so responsible for Billie and her husband, but mostly for Billie, I had this crazy feeling of being married to two women. I felt responsible for two women. I felt like I was going crazy, but I did not ever identify that I was inappropriately attached to Billie and her husband. I was so locked into my old patterns that I was deaf and blind to the truth.

In desperation, I began to pull away from the Verklers, and they could sense it. I had wounded Charlotte with the time I spent away from her. Even though the dissertation was completed in the fall of 1993, things were going downhill rapidly. Charlotte was not happy; the board was equally unimpressed. I felt that I was not measuring up to what Billie and Dr. Verkler wanted, and I experienced phenomenal failure on all relational fronts.

Eventually, things came to an end. The Verklers were aware of the stress that the relationship was placing on me, and they felt the tension between Charlotte and me. It was as if I had been plunged into an ice bath. I awoke suddenly to what was happening and finally told them that I would not be able to work with them anymore. I felt sad and torn, but I knew I had hurt Charlotte deeply. She was at the end of her rope, and I realized that it was time to confront my behavior and end the relationship with the Verklers, even though I would be pulling away from them just like all the others had. The reality is that I was betraying Charlotte with the overextended commitment I had made to them. I had to face myself.

My toxic sense of overresponsibility was so deep that again it almost destroyed my marriage. In the time that followed, I wondered how something so good as wanting to help people could have such potentially devastating side effects. Some therapists who are reading this might label this as a co-dependent relationship. I can accept that. I felt responsible to give Billie the recognition I believed she deserved.

On the brink of receiving my doctorate degree in Personality, Religion, and Culture, I felt more of a failure in my marriage and in my work than I had ever dreamed I could. How was this possible? I was working harder than I had ever worked before, and yet I was doing damage to the people I loved the most. My personal boundaries were terribly out of line. I had the knowledge, but I didn't have the power to emotionally pull out of this by myself. I needed help.

I met with my mentor and closest friends for feedback: Charlotte, Jim and Louine Woodroof, and each of my children. I asked them to tell me how they were experiencing me. They were kind, respectful, affirming of my heart and gifts, but clearly stated they experienced me as having inappropriate boundaries when it came to caring for my family.

I was guilty, and I knew it. My best intentions, my knowledge of personality through all these years, my seeking of God, and the feedback I got from my family and friends left me in an undeniable and convicted place of failure in the relationships I claimed to be most committed to loving.

Every single day I had a mountain to climb. On the mountain, the mystical presence of a loving God could deal with me. Choosing to believe in the massive love of God for me personally had been at the core of my healing. But there was a false faith rooted in my childhood core beliefs that hid a pride in me that said I ought to be able to be good enough to hold everything together.

For the first time, I felt the possibility that Charlotte and I might not make it. That scared me and caused me to want to know even more what was in me that would allow me to push my most cherished relationship to the brink of disaster.

After I told Billie and Dr. Verkler that I would not be working with them again, after I defended my doctoral dissertation, and after the family meeting was done, I was left to ponder what to do next.

In December, Charlotte went away for a few days, and I had time for solitude and space. Two books gave me the food for thought I needed.

Chapter 14 of Richard Foster's book *Prayer* suggests that we *regularly* take a day for nothing but contemplation and solitude. We should just rest and reflect on God's love and presence, our stories, and our spiritual journeys, looking back at the gifts and promises of love that are already ours. I did that. Then I read my professor's book *Taking on the Gods* again with fresh eyes and ears. Dr. Jordan explores the ways our internal gods rule the human heart. I got fifty pages into it and was reminded of the insight I received earlier when reading M. Scott Peck's book.

The light bulbs went on in every part of my being when I remembered Jordan saying that the way you help a neurotic personality is to have the individual identify his belief system, name it, and turn from it. I immediately asked out loud the following question: "What is my core belief?" I answered the following without hesitation: "I believe I am responsible for significant others, and if I can't help them, I am responsible to see to it that they get help!"

"What was working at the core of my being was my determination to be Christ to wounded and broken people."

Then I asked out loud: "Where did you get this?" And I answered, "When you were eight years old and your parents divorced, you took the responsibility to take care of your daddy."

I gasped internally. In the field of psychotherapy this is called the "parentified child"—the child feels responsible for taking care of the parent.

I finally got it. What was working at the core of my being was my determination to be Christ to wounded and broken people. This determination was wrapped in the lie that I could do so. Billie was gifted but unacknowledged by the community. I was going to make sure that I did not abandon her; I would keep my word. I would be the one person in her life who accepted her in the same way that Jesus did. The burden was on me.

I couldn't save her, just as I had been unable to save Mama or Daddy. The truth is, Billie wasn't asking me to save her; that interpretation was coming from inside me. As a child, I had felt responsible to take care of my family. My security was in being the good boy, the one who was strong, friendly, and hardworking. If I could just make life better for Daddy, then he would feel better, I would get to be with him, and he would be able to take care of me. Fear and grief had ahold of me, and I felt the loss of my brothers and sister. Daddy was my lifeline, but he needed help. Meeting his needs became my unconscious childhood priority.

But I couldn't save my family, I couldn't keep the people from falling off my wagon along the way, I couldn't guarantee those I counseled would be healed, and I couldn't rescue Billie. I believed unconsciously that I was responsible, but *I was wrong*.

The lie at the core of my being was that it was up to me—that I must rescue her, that my worth depended on being the one person who could be counted on. What had begun as an attempt to survive childhood trauma had turned into a hidden, toxic pride that was strangling life out of me and those close to me.

"I named it. I brought it out into the open. I literally turned my back on this lie."

I named it. I brought it out into the open. I literally turned my back on this lie. In the next three days of contemplating this in solitude, I crafted a letter of resignation from the position of director of the Family Life and Counseling Center. I knew in every part of me that things had to change, both internally and externally, for me to heal and come to grips with the next step in my life with Charlotte.

But didn't my faith overcome these weaknesses? No. I had built my faith around them. I followed Christ with more zeal than others, served with fewer breaks, and dedicated myself to being a visibly great Christian. Yes, my faith was real, but I was no different from the disciples who were with Jesus for three years and missed the point. They betrayed him in the end. They sat in their shame when Christ came to them and said, "Peace." I felt that I had missed the point, and I had been banking on my goodness to secure me. I would have to accept the grace of God on the same terms given to the Apostle Peter and all the rest who betrayed Jesus.

The world is full of children who are suffering. Across the planet this very day, there are children who are victims of war, who are struggling, who are oppressed and downtrodden. I was one of those children, suffering under broken patterns of thoughts, at war with a false god within me, oppressed by my failings and mistakes. I was a child who happened to be in his fifties, and I was not alone.

Little children interpret the world around them and see the world through tinted glasses. This interpretation is a child's interpretation, but it feels right even when you are an adult. In my life, you can see how toxic these beliefs were, even though I was working as a therapist. *I remained a child in relation to my own life.* I recalled every incident and episode that supported my view of the world, and I continued to respond to others as I did when I was a child. So I was ignorant when it came to relationships, blind to the damage I was causing to Charlotte and the children.

This was the greatest wound that I inflicted on Charlotte and the children. I was wrong, and I could not see it. Charlotte is an amazing woman to have been able to put up with my overresponsible false self and still be supportive on the other side of this emotional-relational brokenness. I know that it is only by the grace of God, as well as Charlotte's love for God and for me, that we were able to make it through this deeply painful and dark time in our marriage. My intent had been to love God, love Charlotte, and love my girls. But I failed.

When Charlotte returned from her trip, I showed her the letter of resignation. She was gracious, but she was concerned about what would come next. I assured her that at fifty-one years of age, I was still marketable. She trusted God, and she loved and trusted me. For the first time in a long time I felt a deep sense of freedom. I called Merle Jordan on the phone with more excitement and joy than when I completed the defense of my doctoral work. I felt like a new man, and I wanted to thank him for his great work and for writing it in a way that made such good sense. I felt like this was the greatest breakthrough in my life.

Through the years I had stayed in a relationship with Rusty Bloodworth and Jim Harding. After our days working with students at the University of Memphis, Rusty had served in the Marines, done graduate work at Yale, married, and since the late 1970s been part of a small house church in Memphis called Servants of Christ. Jim Harding and I met while at Harding. He had been an intern with me in the late seventies. Jim went on to establish a printing company in Memphis, and I had connected him with Rusty when Jim moved to Memphis. Both men were dear friends living in Memphis. They were supportive and loved Charlotte, my children, and me. When they heard of my decision to resign without knowing what I would be doing next, they made it possible for me to take a sabbatical for a year while I worked things out. Over the next several months, I worked in Memphis a couple of days a week with Jim's company and his employees, as well as with the small house church that had formed in 1978.

With the support of Jim and Rusty, as well as the chance to share the journey with the Servants, I entered a new phase of life. I faced the toughest hidden truths about myself that surfaced, and learning these realities allowed my fifties and sixties to be the best years of my life. I discovered an even deeper joy on the journey and finally knew what it was like for the burden to be lifted.

Looking back, I can now see that one other ingredient kept Charlotte and me together—the fact that all our married life we have practiced the art of gazing in the same direction and talking, sharing, confessing, forgiving, and loving one another unconditionally the way God loves us. *Forgiveness is the great miracle we live with, and it is made easier through this rich emotional life that we have cultivated.*

PART FIVE

Even the darkness will not be dark to you;
the night will shine like the day,
for darkness is as light to you.

—Psalm 139:12

CHAPTER TWELVE

I Can See

1994–2004

WE FELT recalibrated and renewed. As my sabbatical continued, three job possibilities surfaced. One offer came from Rochester College (formerly Michigan Christian College), inviting me to join as assistant to the president and serve as spiritual adviser and support for faculty and students. Another came from my friend Jim in Memphis, who had cosupported me throughout the sabbatical. He invited me to join his company full time as a personnel enrichment consultant. The third, and least appealing to me, came from the Woodmont Hills church in Nashville, which was looking for someone to develop community through small groups.

I wanted to stay in Memphis. After all, I was born in the city, I started my work there, and I still had family and close friends there. I would be near my birth mother as well as the Lynn family who had adopted us into their family, and we could worship with the Servants of Christ. We felt as though we belonged with them and shared their passion for putting the kindness and love of Christ into action where they were needed most. Besides, Jim was offering me more money, which would be a big help with children in college.

I met with Rusty before going to Nashville for the interview. We talked through the three choices and prayed together: "Lord, if there is any information I need to know that I do not know or am not aware of at this point, open my eyes to it."

Once I was at the interview in Nashville, I was handed the job description. It ran to three pages, and I told them exactly what I thought: "This job description is a mess. It doesn't leave any room for change. I don't see how I could do it."

Rubel Shelly was the pulpit minister, and people were flocking to hear him each Sunday. It was a thriving church that seemed to be attracting many people who had been wounded by their religion. Many of them were sick of stale religious doctrines and were attracted by the truth of the grace and kindness of God. I quickly knew that I loved the direction of the community and found that their leaders (called shepherds) were compassionate and not abusing their authority. Yet the job description was convoluted, and I was clearly not suited to deliver everything they wanted. But I believed that there might be potential for both of us if only we could figure it out.

With counsel, I proposed an alternative job description, focusing on what I knew I could deliver and what I thought they really needed. In my mind, there was great potential within the church, and if leaders could be raised up rather than having a single therapist to take on everybody, the results could be exciting. Besides, after Searcy I no longer wanted to be a therapist.

The church offered me the job. What's more, as I talked and thought about things, it was clear that if I had gone with my first choice and stayed in Memphis, I could have been repeating history. The overresponsible Messiah Complex pattern might well have kicked in just as it did in Searcy, only instead of my rescuing an outsider, I would be the representative voice of the individual within a for-profit company. But in Nashville, I would be part of a team and one step removed from the action that had caused me so much trouble before by virtue of the fact that I would be training leaders. In Nashville, no one knew my history of overresponsibility. It was one more chance to start again.

Both Charlotte and I felt good about the choice, and there were many moments when we felt the move was confirmed. One of the most precious moments came when we were looking for a home in the area. Mama Sherrill Lynn, who was sixty-eight years old at the time, came with us to look for a place. When she walked in the front door of an old farmhouse in the middle of Nashville on a dead-end street, she said, "This is it." We cherished her presence and her opinion and ended up buying the house. It has been our home since

1994, a place to which our ten grandchildren love to come and play.

As we moved in, we did so with fewer children in tow than we had for years. Sara and Missy had graduated and married. Margy was in undergraduate school, and Elizabeth was ten years old going into the fifth grade. It truly felt like a new beginning.

"Finally, I had begun to understand why my over-responsibility was so harmful."

It is not hard to see why I was so excited about the fresh start Nashville represented. I was finally able to name the enemy, identify my weaknesses, and go about working with people without the shadows of my former errors over me.

Finally, I had begun to understand why my overresponsibility was so harmful. It showed great disrespect to the person who was looking for help when I elevated myself above him or her inappropriately. As I had seen so many times, it also created a co-dependent relationship that can only hinder an individual's personal growth. I learned to see the way I had fed both my pride and my need for affirmation, even though I also genuinely wanted to help. Finally, it became clear to me that by letting my Messiah Complex run wild, the incentive for others to become more dependent on God was lessened. Even if they wanted to, all too often they were unable to make their way to God when I was standing in God's place within the relationship.

Meanwhile, Daddy was dying. He had distanced himself from me since Mama resurfaced. My reconnecting with her was his main complaint. I also had befriended Mary, my stepmother. But there were other things: he had experienced me as self-righteous when I had confronted him earlier about having an affair behind Mary's back.

But he was living in Florida and losing a long battle with cancer. I paid him a visit that lasted three weeks. I knew these were his last days, and I desperately wanted to communicate the grace and love of God to him. I prayed, asking for guidance and the words to say. All I got was that I ought to apologize for judging him. So I did, using the type of language that Daddy would understand.

I was able to pray with him, sing to him, and help him visualize God's love. He had been a regular church attendee as a young teenager, but his guilt and shame about how things had ended up with Mildred and Mary had scarred him. To my mind, that was the reason for his drinking—a failed way of dealing with the pain that came from knowing how much he had let people down. We brought him home from the hospital after a couple of weeks; he and his wife were then living with my sister Carol. He died in Carol's home, surrounded by family.

Mama's death was different. Through the years of reconnecting with her, I saw just how far she was from being healed. But a year before she died, she was in the hospital having some kind of treatment. She was quiet, all alone, and had a vision of God. He was sitting in the room in front of her, with a long flowing white beard and gown, arms outstretched, and a twinkle in his eye. He invited her to join him. That one moment was such a significant encounter that, for the first time ever in her life, she understood that she could be forgiven for all the wrong things she had done—for leaving her children, for cheating on her husband, for doing all the other things. She finally knew it, deep in her gut. On the day she died, Charlotte, my sister, close friends, and I sang to her. For forty-five minutes as we sang, her breathing slipped in and out of a regular rhythm, and we watched as she moved on from this life that she had found so hard.

"For the first time ever in her life, she understood that she could be forgiven for all the wrong things she had done."

In studying Jesus, I learned to marvel at the way *he* built community around him. He met with people in small groups of twelve, put them in twos and threes, and invited them to meet with him alone. When I began my work in Nashville, I shared with the leadership at Woodmont Hills that I believed by using Jesus' model, we could figure out together how to go forward. One leader with whom I grew close was Bob Hooper. Bob was a history professor and one of the shepherd leaders at the church. We met weekly for about two hours, discussing, praying, and seeking understanding for new ways of connecting the story of Jesus to the journey of the church family.

"In studying Jesus, I learned to marvel at the way he built community around him."

I had grown up within the Church of Christ community, worked and studied at a Church of Christ school (Harding), and now attended and worked for a Church of Christ in Nashville, but I remained somewhat ignorant of its history. Bob was able to fill in the gaps in my knowledge, especially when it came to one of the early pioneers, David Lipscomb.

Bob told me how Lipscomb met with small groups and read the Gospel accounts to people, leaving them captivated by the life of Jesus and his story. Bob and I focused on how to get back to the structure that Jesus modeled of building close friendships with disciples.

After prayer and lots of discussion, we came up with a plan. I would meet with the shepherd leaders to listen to their personal stories. I wanted them to better understand their personal journeys and see how God had pursued them in their early years. Drawing on my training at Boston University and the genogram work of psychiatrist Murray Brown, I developed a tool I called Life Markings: Your Core Story. (See more about this at the end of the book.) This simple tool was designed to assist people in mapping the past while looking toward the future. I used a whiteboard to illustrate their journeys, showing the significant relationships—both good and bad—that dominated their lives.

I wanted them to see all the people God had used to communicate his love for them. Processing their journeys also would help them identify their core beliefs around security and survival, affection and esteem, and power and control. I knew only too well that false beliefs in these critical areas, when developed before the age of twelve, would resurface and ultimately sabotage a person when under stress as an adult. How could we keep these beliefs from paralyzing us and damaging our loved ones? Understanding our stories was the first step. Working with the leadership at Woodmont Hills was the place to begin.

I hosted retreats for leaders and others in the church, all the time encouraging people to share their stories with one another. Eighty people were identified as potential small-group leaders. We asked people to spend a month in prayer about joining a small group. We held more training classes. Rubel Shelly delivered talks on experiencing God, and we prayed and prayed and prayed and prayed. By the end of this period of focused prayer, five hundred people had signed up to join a small group. Friendships flourished, and the Spirit was clearly moving. We worked hard, but it was God who fired their imaginations.

"All along we kept the focus on Christ and his role in the worship community."

It was good to come to a place where my position was not as the counselor, but I could help the leaders think through ways of helping people develop healthy, genuine, life-enhancing friendships. It caused me to look inward and determine what I knew beyond a doubt to be true.

All along we kept the focus on Christ and *his* role in the worship community. We talked about God's story, as well as our own, nothing more. The result was that the Holy Spirit showed what he can do when we follow Jesus clearly and deliberately; over a period of ten years, our church community grew from 1,100 to about 2,700.

CHAPTER THIRTEEN

I Want to Move from Life to Life

2012

IN SOME ways this life is full of trouble. The years go by, and the troubles get in line, waiting to strike. Within the opening few months of 2012 I lost five dear friends—all dead. Ranging from eighteen to ninety years old, these people were gone, and I could do nothing to change the fact. I would never see them again with human eyes. I would never talk with them, hear them, or touch their hands at the end of a prayer. Suddenly, my old Messiah Complex seemed to be futile and weak, laughable even. I'd spent much of my life trying to save people through my efforts, but I was clearly powerless when it came to death.

Mo Mantus was seventy-three years old when he died, taken by cancer. I was with him until a few minutes before his last breath. Then there was sweet Janice Hall. She was sixty-eight years old and our neighbor of eighteen years. Precious Jane Swiggart made it to age ninety-two before she died. My dear friend Bill Frey, seventy-two years old, died in Vero Beach, Florida. I arrived four hours before his death and was able to be with Bunny, his wife, and their daughter, Melissa. But the hardest one of all was my precious friend Ty Osman II. Ty II was only eighteen. But you know that by now.

So death was too present at the start of 2012—the very time when I was thinking back over all the years and people who had gone before as I prepared to write this book. I hated what death did to the families I knew and loved, and I hated what death did to me, how it drew me to people but left me mute. At every bedside, in every hospital, at every funeral, and in every parking lot where people stood around dressed in black and looking pale, I was compelled to speak. But what could I say? Where were the words? Where was the language I needed?

I began to see death as a disguise artist, an impostor who tricked his way into all manner of situations and circumstances. He was there in the decay of relationships, the suffocation of hope, the exhaustion of good intentions. I could see in my own story how it shaped and changed me.

Death has been so much a part of my life, from the loss of good friends like Martha and Bob to the passing of my parents. But as age has seasoned me I've come to see death differently. I used to feel overwhelmed by it, but not so much now. When I was a younger man—one desperate to keep people happy and fix things that weren't mine to fix—death was the ultimate slap in the face, the unscalable hurdle, the unfixable problem. I was powerless to help, and I knew it. No wonder it spun me out.

"I know that the death of the body is not the end of the story."

Yet these days I know my enemy, and I know how strong the temptation is to act out of my misguided Messiah Complex. I know that the death of the body is not the end of the story; the story is held by bigger hands than mine. Besides, there's another type of death that I have grown not just to accept but to love: *death to self.* My hopes, my goals, and my gifts are at their best when I'm using them in service to God's agenda, not mine.

Although death played such a big part of life at this time, it was always eventually followed by reflections on life. Yes, I could look back and see the chaos and the sorrow, the difficulties that I had faced. But I could also see the hope. I could always see healing. I could always see the work of the Wounded Healer, Jesus Christ.

So while it might feel as though life is a series of struggles, I do not believe that to be the whole story. There is more to say, always more, and to me, it always comes back to the man they called Jesus. Because of who he was and how he lived, a journey like mine can be changed for the better. Don't get me wrong. My journey is nothing special, nothing unusual. In fact, I think it is universal; everyone shares it—even you. All of us were born to parents who were ill-equipped. What parent could be perfect? What parent could never fail his or her child? What parent could leave no wound?

We all are children, even the ones who are taking their final breaths in well-staffed hospitals surrounded by generations of their offspring. We all are children, struggling to find the right way, stumbling across the wrong path, making mistakes, getting put right, and starting over again. We all are children, all in need of a parent who can and will reach out and offer us the unconditional, unrelenting, and unbreakable love that will soothe our troubled souls. We all are children, and we all need our Father's love.

In the middle of this period of hospital visits and funerals, Charlotte and I made a long-planned visit to Israel. The Holocaust museum in Jerusalem added even more shock and thoughts on death, but there was so much about the Holy Land that I did not stay in that frame of mind for long. There among the dust and the olive trees, on mountainsides, and by inland seas, I began to see more clearly. I was able to sit with nine precious people and to listen with care to each one's life history. Two were children of Holocaust survivors. Another was Norma Gelman Sarvis.

Mount Zion rose in front of us as we sat on the honey-colored stone patio with Norma and her husband, Martin. The air was clean, the sun was bright, and the color of their apartment gleamed in the clear light. Off to my right and at a distance were the Mount of Olives and the Garden of Gethsemane. Little children played in the courtyard.

I thought back to the University of Memphis, 1970, when I met the young Jewish college student Norma Gelman from Greenwood, Mississippi. At the time, Norma was beginning to process the question of Jesus' claim to be the Messiah. She became a part of a group I was leading on campus. She phoned me one day to say that her father found out that she visited a church. He told her if she ever went into a church again, he would kill himself. Norma went home for a visit, and as she walked into the door of the clothing store her father owned, he was opening the mail he'd received from the university. The letter listed her grades as well as her church preference: Christian. Now, forty years later, seated 6,500 miles from where we first met, Norma and I were thankful that her dad never committed suicide and that she and Martin were "in the Land."

Later, as we made the two-hour drive from Jerusalem to Galilee, I kept thinking how long it must have taken Jesus to walk it. We stopped in the desert country to stare at the land where Jesus must have gone after his baptism. No real shelter, very little life—it is hard to imagine a more desolate place to be alone and without food for forty days. We traveled to Ein Gev, to the eastern side of the Sea of Galilee. I could see all the way across the lake to Tiberias and northward to the city of Capernaum. All the biblical stories set around the Sea of Galilee came to mind, as if I were sharing in Christ's memories of the beautiful places and the things that happened to him in the area. I felt like I was coming home.

"I discovered new things as I sat in the sand, seeing the life of Jesus through fresh eyes."

I discovered new things as I sat in the sand, seeing the life of Jesus through fresh eyes. In the ruins of Capernaum, I stared at the synagogue where Jesus taught, and I wondered where Peter lived. We sat on a hillside believed to be where Jesus delivered the Sermon on the Mount. It was such a beautiful place. Then down to Tiberias, across the sea to eat dinner on the western shore. As we ate, we shared our favorite story of Jesus that took place on these rocks and by this water.

So many of our stories were of Jesus offering healing to people. He healed those who were not just physically ill but mentally ill. He healed the outcast and the outsider, those with power and those without. He took on decay and replaced it with life. He faced the darkness and filled it with light.

Seventy years into my story, and I know my story shares this same thread. I was wounded; I was broken. I walked with such a limp that at times it felt as if my very bones had twisted beneath me. *But Jesus continues to heal me.* Not instantly and not with a great flash of lightning or a crash of thunder. *Just the constant reminder of his great love, communicated to me daily through Scripture, prayer, the love and lessons that I soaked in from others.* From darkness to light.

CHAPTER FOURTEEN

I Am Awake

MARCH 9, 2012

It is 4:16 a.m. I am awake, sitting behind my desk in our house that was once surrounded by fields and cows. These days the house shares the land with our neighbors, but the setting is no less tranquil, especially at 4:16 a.m. This is the time when the birds start to sing their dawn chorus, filling the sky with sounds long before the sun fills it with light. I rarely miss these moments, and they are as much a part of my day as eating and sleeping, talking and listening. It seems to me that these moments each morning are about as pure and beautiful and fresh as a newborn baby. Both bring such joy to my heart and breath to my lungs.

My time at Woodmont Hills has been characterized by moments like these—times when I have learned to sit in the stillness and listen to the chorus that surrounds me. Perhaps all those years ago I would have wanted to go out and feed the birds by hand, to care for them and ensure that they would be alive and in full health to sing again tomorrow. But not now. I have learned that I am not quite that responsible.

The same has been true of my work. After things went so wrong in Searcy, I decided not to act as a therapist again. I stuck to that decision as best I could here in Nashville, but then I met Leslie. She was a remarkable young woman who needed help, but she did not need a superhero. As we worked—talking and praying—I found that a new story was being written within me. I felt compassion toward her and wanted to do what I could to help her open up to God's divine healing in her life, but I modulated the intensity of my caring. Her story did not overwhelm my own; it just found its right place. I was not the one who was going to heal her. God was.

These days are different, and I am so grateful to God for the chance to change and grow. And I'm grateful that I am still able to play tennis, for the sport has taught me well. I have been on the court since I was twelve. No one coached me. I just brought the baseball hand-eye coordination and picked up the racket. I had to make a few adjustments, which I did as I watched other and better tennis players in action. Some of those old baseball habits simply did not work on the court, but they were hard for me to shift. So I suppose it was no surprise to anyone who was watching that I lost an early match at the state tournament during high school.

"I am so grateful to God for the chance to change and grow."

I engaged with others in relationships like I played tennis. I was doing my best and was striving to be good enough as a husband, father, leader, and friend. Yet I was incapable of matching reality to my aspirations. As significant relationships began to break down, I knew something was wrong, but I did not know what.

In 1986, I had a one-off lesson with a tennis coach. In thirty minutes, he taught me how to do a topspin backhand, but to do so he had to strip out the problems. He watched my failed attempts at the stroke, observing the patterns my body was going through. He looked at how I was holding the racket, the position of my feet, and basic things that were keeping me from performing the stroke that had eluded me for years. He gave me simple, clear instructions, and I began to practice this new way. With my mistakes exposed, I now had new patterns to learn and new movements to make. In time, my backhand became consistently strong and reliable.

"I now had new patterns to learn and new movements to make."

In my thirties, forties, and fifties, I needed a lot of dismantling. I needed my mistakes and errors to be exposed so I could strip them out and establish new patterns and movements in my life. And if there is one character in the Bible whom I have come to cherish and respect as a result, it is Peter.

Peter had the gaping wound and the failed backhand. He was hotheaded, forgetful, and the most articulate and elaborate of all in his denial of Jesus. He had been with Christ, shown how committed he was, declared himself ready to die for his Master, and stood in judgment of his companion followers. How could he be so blind? How could he go from such personal and intimate interaction with Jesus to saying out loud, "I never knew the man"? There must have been something deep within him that caused such betrayal, something hidden deep in his soul that he was unable to see.

There was also something hidden in my soul, which I could not see. I had failed just like Peter. I made promises I could not keep, missed the point, and hurt the very people who were the closest to me. *I was—I am—wounded, but I am not alone.* There is an army of us out here, the walking wounded, led out from our caves and hospital wards by the One who bears more scars than all of us combined. We are walking wounded whose steps testify to the great mercy of our Healer, cracked vessels whose gaps allow the light to shine through. We are wounded, but we are not alone.

I need to remember this every day, but especially today, *for today we bury Ty II.* It is March and the air is cold. Ty II's funeral is about to begin, and I file through the white church doors along with the others. So many people are here, more than the church can hold. There are overflow rooms filling up already. How can the church hold their grief if it cannot even hold all their bodies?

We sing together, a choir that sounds more like an army. We sing of God's great faithfulness, of amazing grace, of the rose trampled on the ground. We sing that it is well with our souls, when our tears suggest otherwise. How can this be well with anyone's soul? *How can it be well to be here like this?*

But we sing because that is what we do. With our cracked voices and mismatched melodies we are fragile and we are broken, and there is something so beautiful about that. All of us are broken and wounded when compared to the one person who chose to put life right again. Compared to Jesus, the Son of God, we are all struggling. And it is only thanks to Jesus that we can hold on to any hope at all.

Is it well with my soul? If it is, it can only be well because God has made it so. It can only be well because there are an offer of healing and an offer of hope. It can only be well because of God's goodness, not because of my strength to get through this pain and sorrow. *If it is well with my soul, it is only because of him.*

I look down at the order of service again. There, in my hand, is my prompt:

Celebration of Life—Terry Smith

It is time for me to speak, to stand up in front of all these people and tell them what I celebrate about Ty II's life. I have so many words to say, so many lessons I learned from this remarkable young man, and yet I do not know if I will get through it. After all, I had known him since we had moved to Nashville, and he was a year old. Charlotte and I got to know his parents within the church community. We became part of their lives and a small group that met weekly in their home. Later on, Ty II and I went on mission trips together. He and I also played tennis together—and I beat him. We had mutual respect for each other, and I felt we had a bond, as if I was his uncle. I was a regular speaker for the youth group's summer camp, and Ty II and I met one midnight under the stars and talked about God, life, girls, and relationships.

All my life I have believed that if I can just be strong enough and show no weakness, I will succeed. I have believed that I have been responsible for others and that I can say the right things to help people through their darkest nights. Well, right now I do not want to appear to be strong and I do not want to be super responsible and I do not want to have to try to say the right things. I don't want to be that version of Terry. I just want to be the me I know best: the child, the child of God.

I pause on the way up to the microphone and kneel before Ty and Nancy. "I don't think I can do this," I say quietly to them.

Ty lays his hand on me. "Yes, you can."

After I have spoken and the service has ended, we move outside. Later someone tells me more than 1,700 people are here, yet the silence we make together is profound. Nobody speaks as we walk toward the graveside. The air is still cool, but the sun tries to burn its way through to us. The cold wins out.

There are seats for the family in front of the grave and a large pile of earth with two shovels by it. And there is Ty II's casket. Then there are all these people, gathered in silence as the final prayers are said and the casket is lowered into the ground. One by one people step up, reach for a shovel, and pitch earth from the pile down into the hole. Ten, fifteen, twenty minutes pass, all in silence.

Finally Ty II's father is the last to step up. He throws the dirt onto the grave and then tosses the shovel to the ground. "Done," he says.

This young man's life—so full of joy, so delightful, so strong, so giving, so passionate for life, and so caring for others—is now gone. But to what? To death? Not the way I see it. Ty II went from life to life.

I am getting old now, so old that Charlotte, my daughters, and I talk about life after my passing without fear. We talk about the memories we have made and the memories we will choose to hold on to. *We talk about passing from life to life, from darkness to light.*

If I know one thing from writing this book, it is this: for too long I was surer about life after death than I was about life before death. I knew and trusted and tried to follow Jesus, but it took a long time before I allowed him to tend to the wounds within me that I had tried so hard to hide. It was only then that I learned what it means to live.

What does it mean? It means being free—free to admit that the wounds need tending, free to admit that we are imperfect, free to admit that our failings hold us back. It also means being free to follow Jesus, no matter how great the risk. It means being free to put aside the hurt and the pain. It means tossing the shovel down and saying, "Done." All that mess, all that dirt, the wounds and those failures of mine, they are the past me. I choose to live love and forgiveness, the light of life that God provides.

As the service finished at the graveside, Ty II's sisters released three white doves—Father, Son, and Holy Spirit. Then Ty II's parents released one more dove into the sky to represent their son. We watched the bird as it flew higher, its wings taking it in broad sweeps across the sky. So much life and freedom in that tiny body. So much care. So much hope.

Epilogue

EACH OF us is responsible for how we choose to live in this world. I will close with this example of choosing to believe in an unseen world where forgiveness and joy are the center of reality. I have so much to learn, so much to give and a desire to love fully to the end. Yes, I believe in an unseen world. This story told by Henri Nouwen and adapted by Wayne Dyer best illustrates two different worldviews:

> Imagine this scene if you will. Two babies are in utero, confined to the wall of their mother's womb, and they are having a conversation. For the sake of clarity we'll call these twins Ego and Spirit.
>
> Spirit says to Ego, "I know you are going to find this difficult to accept, but I truly believe there is life after birth."
>
> Ego responds, "Don't be ridiculous. Look around you. This is all there is. Why must you always be thinking about something beyond this reality? Accept your lot in life. Make yourself comfortable and forget about all of this life-after-birth nonsense."
>
> Spirit quiets down for a while, but her inner voice won't allow her to remain silent any longer. "Ego, now don't get mad, but I have something else to say. I also believe that there is a Mother."
>
> "A Mother!" Ego guffaws. "How can you be so absurd? You've never seen a Mother. Why can't you accept that this is all there is? The idea of a Mother is crazy. You are here all alone with me. This is your reality. Now grab hold of that cord. Go into your corner and stop being so silly. Trust me, there is no Mother."
>
> Spirit reluctantly stops her conversation with Ego, but her restlessness soon gets the better of her. "Ego," she implores, "please listen without rejecting my idea. Somehow I think those constant pressures we both feel, those movements that make us so uncomfortable sometimes, that continual repositioning and all of that closing in that seems to be taking place as we keep growing, is getting us ready for a place of glowing light, and we will experience it very soon."

"Now I know you are absolutely insane," replies Ego. "All you've ever known is darkness. You've never seen light. How can you even contemplate such an idea? Those movements and pressures you feel are your reality. You are a distinct separate being. This is your journey. Darkness and pressures and a closed-in feeling are what life is all about. You'll have to fight it as long as you live. Now grab your cord and please stay still."

Spirit relaxes for a while, but finally she can contain herself no longer. "Ego, I have only one more thing to say and then I'll never bother you again."

"Go ahead," Ego responds impatiently.

"I believe all of these pressures and all of this discomfort is not only going to bring us to a new celestial light, but when we experience it, we are going to meet Mother face-to-face and know an ecstasy that is beyond anything we have ever experienced up until now."

"You really are crazy, Spirit. Now I'm truly convinced of it."

I have discovered that human beings are amazing, wonderful, and intended for life and joy. The universal obstacles that I am experiencing are the injustices, the untimely deaths, and the human failures that lead to despair and the incomprehensible grief where I cannot answer the question of *why*. I was not given a choice of being born, but I am given a choice of how I will love and live in this world.

I discovered the mystery of the toxic beliefs. The beliefs of a twelve-year-old do not work in the world. The "be perfect," "perform to please," "be strong," "be smart," "hide," "be invisible," "be funny," "conform," "help others," "work hard," "be good, "take care of the parent," and other beliefs confront the human personality with an impossible job with devastating failure at the end. However, these beliefs can be overcome.

A lack of forgiveness for myself, when I had to face my great failures, was a huge obstacle. Understanding the false self helped me with that. Then I needed forgiveness for the things that I did do. Real failure, real betrayal, and real evil done by a person are a spiritual problem. I turned to the spiritual to solve my issues with life. Everyone chooses to handle life in a different way. I found a way, and

I wanted to share it with those I love and others who might want to listen. Each person must choose a perspective on how to define reality. I wanted my thought processes to be clear to my children, grandchildren, and friends and to strangers who might choose to search out this path.

I took the road of spiritual transformation with the Psalms being my mother, Proverbs being my father, and the story of Jesus calibrating my soul.

These paths continue to lead me to healing and joy!

• • •

A word about my daughters: When I look at my four daughters, each of whom is an amazing, responsible, loving mother and contributor to the world, my heart overflows with gratitude. The cycle of death has been broken. With authentic joy discovered in the pain I give this story to them, to you, and to all who read a process tested and found true in my lived experience. When I reflect on the mother of these four daughters, Charlotte, I find my soul mate and dearest friend who has stood as the wind beneath my wings over the last forty-eight years.

The Depth of Night

No one knows the depth of night
The darkness that overwhelms
The despair that can destroy
But God has been there

He became like us
Experienced betrayal
He entered the pain
No one understood his grief
Could fully identify

He identified with me
He came to be where I was
I could not come to his world
So he came to mine

He promised to help
He said, "Do not be afraid,
I will not leave you."
He always keeps his promise
Jesus' love will never end.

Terry S. Smith
February 11, 2013

Afterword

Upon completing *Delta Blues*, I'm reminded again of how powerful is the framing of life's direction. For me, that framing revolves around one word: "Yes."

No matter where we are, no matter the darkness, no matter the confusion, no matter the failure, one can resolve to say, "Yes"; to whisper, "Yes"; to cry, "Yes"; to shout, "Yes."

Paul penned the words to the Corinthian church, "All the promises of God find their Yes in him."

Every time I'm with Terry, I experience a life of "Yes." That "Yes" breathes on every page of *Delta Blues*. Terry from very early in his life has moved steadily in the direction of that "Yes." Emerging from the difficult family life in which he grew up, emerging from his personal struggle to find his real self, emerging from encounters with failure, Terry kept saying, "Yes."

And that fierce commitment to "Yes" eventually brought him home to himself, his family, and others.

And he lives among others in ways that help them find their "Yes."

And finally it is the word "Yes" that leads to a life that is well lived, well loved, and well served.

Landon Saunders

Acknowledgments

I had an idea. I wanted to do it. I needed to do it for me. I wanted to do it for my grandchildren and great-grandchildren. I wanted to write this book, but I needed help. A dream has come through because of a community of friends who believed in me, loved me, and worked hard to make it happen. Thanks to writer Craig Borlase for the way he sculpted the volumes of material I sent him on my life story. He helped me boil it down.

Charlotte is my greatest hero. She believed in me. I have experienced God's love through her. She made sure I had the space and time, and she encouraged me to begin. She says, "You have the best episodic memory of anyone I know." She wanted me to write it down.

Thank you to my daughters Sara, Melissa, Margy, and Elizabeth who have loved me, shared great memories, and stand as our greatest legacy of women who love well.

Jim Woodroof critiqued the book and made great suggestions. His agreeing to write the foreword and Landon Saunders writing the afterword are the icing on the cake for me. These two men have been my mentors for more than forty years. They are two of my heroes.

Rusty Bloodworth read this book out loud to his wife, Fran. Their feedback has been invaluable. Rusty said, "You need to do this. It will encourage a lot of people, not just your grandchildren." They have been my greatest encouragers. Thank you to Christopher Bloodworth for his suggestions and fine-tuning of the manuscript.

Dr. Joe McLaughlin, child psychologist and Vanderbilt Professor of Psychology, and Norma Sarvis, teacher of young people for many years from Jerusalem, Israel, were my earliest critics and encouragers.

Cindy Elmore, administrative assistant and friend, has been the steady, daily reader and corrector in this process from the beginning.

Dr. Jean Enochs, friend and educator, assisted in crafting the questions to help readers explore their own stories. Cindy Putnam McMillan spent two intense days working with me to make critical changes.

Bob and Bonnie Hooper, Natalie Allen, Sara Anne Ross, Merle Jordan, Judy Flatt, and Rubel Shelly gave feedback and valuable suggestions. Thank you to Randy and Rhonda Lowry, who told me I needed to write a book. Thank you to Steve Brumfield, who led me through the process of publishing this book, and to Karen Roof, who captured the themes of darkness and light so dramatically on the cover. Thank you to Dimples Kellogg, who brought the book home to the final copy. Thank you all for your friendship and love.

Finally, the board of Coaching: Life Matters have been cheerleaders and financially supported this project. Thank you, Ty Osman, Rusty Bloodworth, Ron Joyner, Steve Brumfield, Joy Mercy Liddle, Kim Hickok, and Richard Jones.

To those who heard about this project and donated to the completion of this work, I thank you, and I thank God. *It is done!*

Appendices

Contemplation is the highest expression of man's intellectual and spiritual life. It is that life itself, fully awake, fully active, fully aware that it is alive. It is spiritual wonder. It is spontaneous awe at the sacredness of life, of being. It is gratitude for life, for awareness, and for being. It is the vivid realization of the fact that life and being in us proceed from an invisible, transcendent, and infinitely abundant Source. Contemplation is, above all, awareness of the reality of that Source.

—*Thomas Merton*

Appendix A

Questions to Help in Exploring Your Story

Chapter 1

1. Can you name friends and families who were important in shaping you as a preschool child?
2. What do you know of the lives of your parents and grandparents, the roles they played and the impact they had on your life?
3. What are the three or four most memorable events of your childhood?

Chapter 2

1. Looking at your childhood, who were you? How did you interact with friends and family?
2. What strengths did your childhood give you? What weaknesses?
3. Can you point to a significant turning point in your young life?

Chapter 3

1. Who and what events were positive forces in your school-aged childhood? The negative?
2. What survival skills did you develop to make it through your childhood?
3. In what ways was religion positive or negative in your childhood?
4. Who and what events were positive forces in your adolescence? The negative?
5. Did church or religious affiliation play any role in your youth? If so, describe that role.

Chapter 4

1. What have you learned about yourself from your academic performance and standing?
2. How did your first work experiences affect your thinking and decisions in life?
3. What early romantic interests were important? How did they affect your self-image?

Chapter 5

1. Were there times of crisis during your young adult life? Have you dealt with them adequately?
2. Can you name some places and situations in which you felt loved and secure?
3. What ideas and events guided your vocational choices?

Chapter 6

1. How have racial and social inequality, national and international conflict, and death affected your life and your life choices?
2. What answers have you found to questions about the meaning and purpose of life, about where human beings are from, and where we are going?
3. How are current relationships with your family of origin affecting your life now?

Chapter 7

1. Can you list the friendships of your life that are the most meaningful to you?
2. Can suffering bring good into your life? How or why not?
3. What did Jesus say were the two most important things to learn from the Hebrew Bible?

Chapter 8

1. Which is more important to you: family or vocation? Are there changes you need to make?
2. In our relationships with others, what are signs that we are pushing rather than aiding? Of being pushed rather than helped to make our own decisions?
3. Explain what is meant by "eating the menu rather than the food." Is this something you have been, or are guilty of, doing? Explain.

Chapter 9

1. What is the most important goal in your life today? Does time spent in your daily life reflect this? What gets in the way of this pursuit?
2. Do you experience joy in your day-to-day life? What brings you joy? What destroys it?
3. How well do you know yourself and your family of origin? What do you need to address?

Chapter 10

1. Have you taken on unwise burdens in your life? How can you best gain freedom from them?
2. How important are your children in your life? Others' children?
3. What are ways you receive guidance from God?

Chapter 11

1. When old habits and patterns of life leave you deaf and blind to the truth, what do you do to gain insight?
2. Where have you experienced the life-giving nature of a loving group of people?
3. Do you seek the opinion of others in the group or discuss life decisions?
4. How do your major goals match with how you spend your time and energy? Do you need to set boundaries or limits?
5. In thinking about the person you are and your family of origin, are there questions you need to ask?

Chapter 12

1. How do you go about making life-changing decisions?
2. Are there members of your family that you may be able to relate to more helpfully?
3. Who are the people in your life who have communicated love to you?
4. Can you state your beliefs concerning the following?
    - Security and survival
    - Affection and esteem
    - Power and control
5. In your life how do you keep your focus on Christ?

Chapter 13

1. Is death or decay threatening any of your relationships, hopes, or good intentions? How can you bring healing to these?
2. How would you explain or restate what is meant by "death to self"?
3. How would you like for Jesus to heal you?

Chapter 14

1. Do you expect to always succeed? How do you respond to failure and losses?
2. Do you know the spiritual One who wants to walk beside and aid you?
3. What are your beliefs and expectations of existence after physical death?

Appendix B

Value of Life Markings: Your Core Story in Listening to a Person's Story

Life Markings: Your Core Story is about listening to the relational history to understand a person's story, particularly the first eighteen years of life. Significant components give a person particular awareness of two important things. First, the person becomes aware of the significant people and events that helped shape the early years. I look for the people who affirmed, loved, and valued the person in the first eighteen years. Second, I listen for the person's core beliefs.

A person makes three major decisions by the age of twelve that have to do with security, significance, and power. Psychotherapists have identified three dimensions of personality: intellect, emotion, and instinct (or head, heart, and gut).These core beliefs a person adopts are powerful drivers of personality, yet they are mostly unconscious. Core beliefs can be both helpful and damaging.

Core beliefs are helpful because children use them to figure out how they will approach the world, and these beliefs are gifts that help them accomplish what they think they want for their lives. Core beliefs can be damaging because they are essentially the beliefs of a twelve-year-old being used by the adult to handle relationships. These early formed core beliefs are often flawed and immature because "children are the world's greatest recorders, but they are the world's worst interpreters."

Life Markings: Your Core Story takes the unseen and unconscious and makes them concrete. This tool raises the awareness of the person and empowers him or her with the ability to decide, as an adult, whether the beliefs adopted as a child are appropriate in adulthood. Here lies the trouble. We find people do not have the tools to cope with life as an adult when they use beliefs of a twelve-year-old to reach their relationship goals. Many people are failing at their most significant relationships because they are not aware they are living by these toxic, immature beliefs. Once they become aware of these core beliefs, they realize they have a choice. They can choose the beliefs of a twelve-year-old or make an adult decision that is appropriate to the situation.

The ancient proverb says, "Though it cost all you have, get understanding." Life Markings: Your Core Story takes the classic genogram that is used in family systems to understand the patterns handed down for generations and makes it an enriching, positive tool to understand the wisdom in everyone's story.

Give someone safety, good information, and time in a confidential group, and he or she will be able to process his or her life story in a meaningful way. The groups are not for the purpose of telling a person how to live but to share stories and listen in a nurturing atmosphere.

The fundamental belief underlying the administration and interpretation of Life Markings: Your Core Story is "there is nothing more important in all the world than a human being" (Landon Saunders).

Appendix C

Family of Origin Questions

1. What is your father's name?
2. What is your mother's name?
3. How many brothers and sisters do you have?
4. Where do you fit? Oldest? Youngest? Middle?
5. Who is the oldest?
6. List children, ages, brothers and sisters from oldest to youngest.
7. If parents are divorced, widowed, remarried, note this along with names of spouse(s).
8. How many brothers and sisters did your father have?
9. What are your paternal grandfather's and grandmother's names?
10. Where does your father fit in? Oldest? Youngest? Middle?
11. How many brothers and sisters did your mother have?
12. What are your maternal grandfather's and grandmother's names?
13. Where does your mother fit in? Oldest? Youngest? Middle?
14. How and when did your maternal grandfather die?
15. Brothers and sisters? Alive or dead?
16. How and when did your maternal grandmother die?
17. What are some descriptive adjectives your father would use to describe his father growing up? (Kind, harsh, etc.)
18. What are some descriptive adjectives your father would use to describe his mother growing up? (Kind, harsh, etc.)
19. What was the relationship between your paternal grandparents? Close? Distant? Conflict?
20. What was your relationship with your father growing up? Close? Distant? Conflict?
21. What are some descriptive adjectives your mother would use to describe her father growing up? (Kind, harsh, etc.)
22. What are some descriptive adjectives your mother would use to describe her mother growing up? (Kind, harsh, etc.)
23. What was the relationship between your maternal grandparents? Close? Distant? Conflict?
24. What are some adjectives you would use to describe how you experienced your mother when you were growing up?

25. What was your relationship with your mother growing up? Close? Distant?

Conflict?

26. What is the relationship between your parents? Close? Distant? Conflict?

27. Describe with adjectives how you experienced your parents growing up.

28. Describe with adjectives how you experienced school growing up.

29. What two or three words would you use to describe the atmosphere of your home? (Examples: secure, loving, fun, empty, tense, insecure, etc.)

30. Describe with adjectives how you experienced religion growing up.

31. Was religion positive or negative for you growing up? Ages 0-12? 13-18?

32. Who affirmed you when you were growing up? Valued you? Took delight in you?

33. After looking at your core story, do you have any personal reflection that gives you any new understanding of your life in this family?

Appendix D

Questions for Discovering Core Beliefs

How would you complete these sentences if you were twelve years old?

Security/Survival
What I learned to do to survive or be secure when I was twelve years old was ________________________________.

Affection/Esteem
What I learned to do to feel affirmed, valued, beloved, or cared for by others was ____________________________.

Power/Control
What I learned to do to control the way others responded to me was ____.

The following are sample responses for each category:

Security/Survival
Be good
Obey
Be perfect
Work hard
Be invisible

Affection/Esteem
Perform to please
Achieve to please
Be the best
Be pretty

Power/Control
Be funny
Be nice
Be cute
Be strong/show no weakness

Appendix E

Words to My Grandchildren and Others

March 5, 2013

My primary inspiration in writing this book was for my grandchildren's children. You are alive now partially because of the choices I made at eighteen years old. I wanted you to know the reason I made the choices and give you a word of wisdom about finding authentic joy on your journey. I hate death and death in relationships that are revealed in my story. I hate what it does to loved ones near. Thank you for taking the time to read. You can know that I prayed for you before you were born. I will look forward to meeting you.

• • •

This book is about real life, my life and how I have traveled it over the last seventy years. I would not change places with any person I have ever known or read about. The following are my closing remarks to you, my grandchildren, and anyone else who chooses to read these words.

I can't let my head rule—that isolates me.
I can't let my heart rule—that judges me.
I can't let my gut rule—that condemns others.

When I engaged all three, I discovered a joy unspeakable. Alone, each level leads to destruction because there are no boundaries to guide me. Using all three dimensions, I am held in check to do what is best for me and for others.

I was challenged in the 1970s to study personality. Proverbs says, "Though it cost all you have, get understanding." In continuing to seek insight into human beings I keep growing in my respect for my life and for others. I have come to believe there is nothing on this planet more important than a person. The cycle of death that was handed down to me has been broken.

Engaging in seeking knowledge and understanding in each of three dimensions has led me to the surprising joy that is available to every person.

Seven Suggestions for You

1. *Choose not to make friends with your pain.* I have learned not to focus on my problems but to see them as opportunities to learn. Through pain and problems, I have discovered a path of hope. Yes, the pain and the problems have created the right questions to engage all three levels of personality—the head, the heart, and the gut. Finding a perspective that interacts on all three levels has been a surprising discovery.

2. *Choose an authentic vision for your life.* At eighteen I knew what I did not want, but I didn't know how to get what I wanted. The first thing I was seeking was peace. I hoped if I ever got married, I would have a home where there was peace. I had never witnessed it in my family. The vision: if I ever got married, I would be on one end of the couch and my wife would be on the other end, and there would be peace. Growing up in my home, I could cut the tension with a knife. I learned that without a vision, the past dictates the future.

3. *Remember those who genuinely love you.* I had those sprinkled throughout my early life with the Roseberry family and the grandmothers. My parents gave the best they could. They were not equipped, as teenagers, to provide a safe, loving home. The life cards I was dealt brought pain and problems. There was a love larger than my pain. That vision of love drew me to begin asking relationship questions.

4. *Take responsibility for your choices.* It was either figure it out or die. Taking responsibility was a survival move. I could feel the darkness of my soul. At the age of eighteen, I discovered I could do evil under certain circumstances. That scared me. I could not trust Mama, Daddy, or religion, and my friends were gone. Taking responsibility in the pain and loneliness created the right questions for me in my desperation. I was dying inside, and my survival instincts surfaced. I was crying out for someone to help me make sense of what was happening to me. Looking back, I can see all three dimensions of my personality kicked in, igniting a fire in me determined to find my way. The song "Climb Every Mountain" became well known through the movie *The Sound of Music.* I sang this song as I climbed the mountain with my questions.

5. *Search out the Wisdom Literature in the Hebrew Scriptures.* At the age of twenty, I began to read and meditate on the Psalms and Proverbs daily. They gave practical advice in relationships and language for the unspoken deep grief of the losses I had experienced. These reflections have illuminated a path through the years.

6. *Pay attention to your questions.*
Who am I?
What am I doing here?
Where am I going?

These were my questions at the age of eighteen. I found no easy answers, formulas, or quick fixes. My quest for meaning has caused me to read extensively, particularly biographies. I read people's life stories and saw how they handled the difficult times in their lives. Dealing with the pain and the problems gave me models I could see. We all face the same universal issues: death, guilt, fear, and despair. Having listened to thousands whisper in my ear their stories, their questions, their deep feelings of hurt, I am compelled to be a presence of hope. The head, heart, and gut confront these issues in me. This search has been mine, and now I want to share the story of what makes sense to me with those dear to me and, I hope, with those with the same quest for meaning.

With all the religions and philosophies giving optional worldviews I settled on one perspective that has been the basis of my personal journey for the last fifty-two years. Because I found no person worthy to guide me, I decided I would do my own research and study historically the man Jesus. Doing this required that I seek more education. That meant I had to learn Hebrew, Greek, and Aramaic to give me access to the original languages of the first-century world. Of course, a person today does not need to learn these languages because of so many reliable translations, but I did not know that then. This became a mountain-climbing challenge as I did not see myself as the brightest bulb in the room. I discovered that my mind was a whole lot better than I thought, though, when I felt my life and future were at stake.

7. *Choose a focus that leads to joy.* I chose to center on the life and teaching of the person of Jesus of Nazareth who claimed to be the coming Messiah. Practicing his teaching and believing his promises of life and even victory over death itself continue to lead me into relationships of authentic joy.

Jesus' life and teaching made sense to me on these fronts:

- I liked the way he treated broken people like me.
- His teaching practiced in relationships works. When we treat people like we want to be treated, each person is respected.
- He dealt with death. I am convinced he was raised from death. This understanding brings hope for our own resurrection and the resurrection of our loved ones.

His words have led me into a daily relationship with the Creator of the universe as my loving, compassionate Father. I am rich with friendships beginning with my wife, children, grandchildren, and dear close friends who are treasured gifts. My life purpose is to love others the way I have been loved—unconditionally. He has taught me the meaning of friendship. A friend is one who is always glad to see you and has no immediate plans for your improvement. His love draws me to want to grow and want to sacrifice to make others' lives better. His love causes me to keep growing, learning, changing, giving, and forgiving.

The greatest miracle of all in this new way of life is forgiveness. Because of him, I am able to forgive myself and others.

To sum it up simply, I found profound wisdom as Psalms mothered me and Proverbs fathered me. The story of Jesus recorded in Matthew, Mark, Luke, and John in what is known as the New Testament has given me understanding and insight revealing the power to live in peace and freedom, regardless of my circumstances.

I grew up in the darkness of human failure. I now arise to the joy of a forgiving God and the power to be transformed.

His answer is "Yes" to every person.

Notes

Foreword

On a December day some years ago, a Florida lawyer with a love for salt water: "The Raptures of the Depths," *Waterloo Daily Courier*, October 16, 1964, 15.

Terry's victory, chronicled in this book, also calls to mind lines from a poem by Owen Seaman: "Between Midnight and Morning," in *Punch*, cited in *Verse for Patriots*, compiled by Jean Broadhurst (Philadelphia: Lippincott, 1919), 288.

Part 1

No one ever told me that: C. S. Lewis, *A Year with C. S. Lewis* (New York: HarperCollins, 2009), 236.

Chapter 3

C. Austin Miles, "I Come to the Garden Alone," 1912.

Chapter 4

one line spoken by Jesus stopped me in my tracks: "I am come that they might have life . . . ," John 10:10 KJV.

The minister mentor had given me these words . . . : *For by these He has granted to us His precious and magnificent promises:* 2 Peter 1:4 NASB.

Part 2

Aim at Heaven and you will get earth "thrown in": C. S. Lewis, *Mere Christianity* (New York: HarperCollins, 2009), 134.

Part 3

You don't get to make up most of your story: Ann Voskamp, "5 Things You Need to Know Before You Begin Your 2nd Term of Life," A Holy Experience, January 21, 2013, http://www.aholyexperience.com/2013/01/5-things-you-need-to-know-before-you-begin-your-2nd-term-of-life/.

Chapter 7

"Terry, do you know the psalm that says, 'Teach us to number our days, that we may gain a heart of wisdom'?": Psalm 90:12 NIV.

I asked him what he meant, and he referred to the letter written by Paul to the Ephesians, which describes the process of putting on the spiritual armor of God: Ephesians 6:10–18.

When Jesus quoted the psalmist as he hung on the cross—"My God, my God, why have you forsaken me?": Psalm 22:1 NIV.

I found a man who spoke about a God who "is near to the broken-hearted and saves those who are crushed in spirit": Psalm 34:18 NASB.

Chapter 9

I took seriously the words of the Apostle John when he wrote, "Those who say they live in God should live their lives as Jesus did": 1 John 2:6 NLT.

Part 4

The past is never dead. It's not even past: William Faulkner, *Requiem for a Nun* (New York: Vintage Books, 1979), speaker was Gowan Stevens, p. 73, act 1.

Chapter 11

What was supposed to run for fourteen weeks ended up carrying on for three years! Details of the group appear in my doctoral dissertation "The Use of Psychodrama in a Conservative Church" for Boston University.

Part 5

Even the darkness will not be dark to you. . . : Psalm 139:12 NIV.

Epilogue

Imagine this scene if you will: Cited in Wayne Dyer, *Your Sacred Self: Making the Decision to Be Free* (New York: HarperCollins, 2009), ix–x.

Afterword

Paul penned the words to the Corinthian church: 2 Corinthians 1:20 ESV.

Appendix

Thomas Merton, *New Seeds of Contemplation* (Abbey of Gethsemani, 1961), 1.

Appendix B

The ancient proverb says, "Though it cost all you have, get understanding": Proverbs 4:7 NIV.

Appendix D

"children are the world's greatest recorders, but they are the world's worst interpreters": David Seamands, *Healing for Damaged Emotions* (Colorado Springs: David C. Cook, 1992), 95.

Suggested Reading

If you would tell me the heart of a man,
tell me not what he reads, but what he rereads.
—*François Mauriac*

Here is a list of books that have influenced me over the years. I encourage you to read them. Of course my daily reading of the Hebrew Scriptures and the New Testament documents has been the most significant influence on me: Psalms being my mother, Proverbs being my father, and the Gospels revealing the heart of compassion through the life and teaching of Jesus Christ.

1957

Dickens, Charles, *A Tale of Two Cities*

1960–1965

Bainton, Roland, *Here I Stand: A Life of Martin Luther*
Bonhoeffer, Dietrich, *Letters and Papers from Prison*, ed. Eberhard Bethge
Frankl, Viktor E., *Man's Search for Meaning*
Gibran, Kahlil, *Jesus: The Son of Man*
Gibran, Kahlil, *The Prophet*
McMillan, E. W., *The Minister's Spiritual Life*
Phillips, J. B., *Your God Is Too Small*
Wisdom Literature: Psalms, Proverbs, Job, Ecclesiastes, and Song of Solomon

1969–1979

Bonhoeffer, Dietrich, *Cost of Discipleship*
Bonhoeffer, Dietrich, *Life Together*
Brother Lawrence, *Practicing His Presence*
Chambers, Oswald, *My Utmost for His Highest*
Drummond, Henry, *The Greatest Thing in the World and Other Essays*
Ijams, E. H., *Power to Survive and Surpass*
Kempis, Thomas à, *Imitation of Christ*
Lewis, C. S., *Chronicles of Narnia*

Lewis, C. S., *Mere Christianity*
Manson, Thomas Walter, *The Servant-Messiah*
McCasland, David, *Oswald Chambers: Abandoned to God*
Muller, George, *Autobiography*
Nee, Watchman, *Sit, Walk, Stand*
Nee, Watchman, *The Normal Christian Life*
Nouwen, Henri, *Wounded Healer*
Schaeffer, Francis, *Escape from Reason*
Schaeffer, Francis, *The God Who Is There*
Seamands, David, *Healing for Damaged Emotions*
Smith, Hannah Whitall, *The Unselfishness of God and How I Discovered It: A Spiritual Autobiography*
Smith, Hannah Whitall, *The Christian's Secret of a Happy Life*
Taylor, Dr. and Mrs. Howard, *Hudson Taylor's Spiritual Secret*
Taylor, Hudson, *The Autobiography of Hudson Taylor: Missionary to China*
Woodroof, Jim, *Aroma of Christ*
Woodroof, Jim, *Between a Rock and a Hard Place*
Woodroof, Jim, *Struggles of the Kingdom*

1979–1989

Crabb, Larry, *Effective Biblical Counseling*
Crabb, Larry, *The Papa Prayer*
Foster, Richard, *Celebration of Discipline*
Jordan, Merle, *Taking on the Gods*
Kelly, Thomas, *Testament of Devotion*
Lucado, Max, *On the Anvil*
MacDonald, Gordon, *Ordering Your Private World*
Nee, Watchman, *Against the Tide*
Packer, J. I., *Knowing God*
Peck, M. Scott, *The Road Less Traveled*
Saunders, Landon, *How to Win Seven Out of Eight Days a Week*

1989–1994

Bowen, Murray, and Michael Kerr, *Family Evaluation*
Foster, Richard, *Prayer*
Friedman, Edwin, *Generation to Generation*
Moreno, J. L., *Writings*
Nouwen, Henri, *Reaching Out*
Nouwen, Henri, *The Return of the Prodigal Son*
Woodroof, Jim, *Church in Transition*

1995–2013

Anonymous, *The Cloud of Unknowing*
Benson, Robert, *Living Prayer*
Benson, Robert, *Writings*
Guinness, Os, *The Call*
Gunther, Margaret, *Holy Listening*
Hallesby, Ole, *Prayer*
Hinson, Glenn, *Spiritual Preparation for Christian Leadership*
Jones, Paul Tudor, *The Chain of Kindness*
Jordan, Merle, *Reclaiming Your Story*
Kang, Joshua Choonmin, *Deep-Rooted in Christ*
Keating, Thomas, and Betty Sue Flowers, *Heartfulness*
Keating, Thomas, *Invitation to Love*
Keating, Thomas, *Open Mind, Open Heart*
Lewis, C. S., various books on his life
Meninger, William, *The Process of Forgiveness*
Merton, Thomas, *The Seven Storey Mountain*
Metaxas, Eric, *Bonhoeffer: Pastor, Martyr, Prophet, Spy*
Mulholland, Robert, Jr., *Shaped by the Word*
Mulholland, Robert, Jr., *The Deeper Journey*
Nouwen, Henri, *Spiritual Direction*
Rohr, Richard, *Falling Upward*
Rohr, Richard, *The Enneagram*
Saunders, Landon, *Life That Loves to Happen . . . No Matter What Happens*
Shelly, Rubel, *I Knew Jesus Before He Was a Christian and I Liked Him Better Then*
Shelly, Rubel, and John York, *The Jesus Proposal*
Tozer, A. W., *The Pursuit of God*
Wiesel, Elie, *Night*
Willard, Dallas, *Renovation of the Heart*
Willard, Dallas, *The Divine Conspiracy*
Willard, Dallas, *Spiritual Disciplines*
Woodroof, Jim, *Famous Sayings of Jesus*
Young, Sarah, *Jesus Calling*